Childhood Anxiety Disorders

Childhood Anxiety Disorders

Ashley J. Smith
Amy M. Jacobsen

MP MOMENTUM PRESS
HEALTH

First published in 2017 by
Momentum Press®, LLC
222 East 46th Street, New York, NY 10017
www.momentumpress.net

ISBN-13: 978-1-94561-230-5 (print)
ISBN-13: 978-1-94561-231-2 (e-book)

Momentum Press Child Clinical Psychology "Nuts and Bolts" Collection

Cover and interior design by S4Carlisle Publishing Services Private Ltd., Chennai, India

First edition: 2017

10 9 8 7 6 5 4 3 2 1

Printed in the United States of America

Abstract

Anxiety disorders affect almost 20 percent of youth at any point in time. Recognizing symptoms, accurately diagnosing, and providing effective intervention are imperative because untreated anxiety disorders are associated with significant comorbidities and functional impairment. Fortunately, there are effective treatments. A discrepancy, however, remains between what practitioners *should* do and what they *actually* do. To help bridge this gap, this book offers a practical "how to" guide that synthesizes research, offers clear explanations of the theoretical underpinnings of cognitive behavioral therapy with specific intervention techniques, illustrated by case examples, and addresses critical topics to boost favorable outcomes.

Keywords

anxiety, anxiety disorders, assessment, cognitive behavioral therapy, cognitive interventions, evidence-based treatment, exposure with response prevention, exposure, medication, obsessive compulsive disorder, relaxation training

Contents

CHAPTER 1

Description and Diagnoses

Anxiety disorders are the most prevalent disorders of childhood, affecting almost 20 percent of youth at any given point in time (Kessler, Chiu, Demler, & Walters, 2005). As such, anyone who works with children, including mental health practitioners, medical professionals, and school personnel, is likely to encounter an anxiety disorder. Recognizing the signs and symptoms, accurately diagnosing, and providing timely and effective intervention are imperative because untreated anxiety disorders may alter the developmental trajectory of the child and result in comorbid depression, substance abuse disorders, increased suicide risk, negative impact on family relationships, academic underachievement, social difficulties, and lower quality of life (e.g., Strauss, Frame, & Forehand, 1987; Woodward & Fergusson, 2001). Fortunately, effective treatments for pediatric anxiety disorders have been established. A discrepancy, however, remains between what practitioners *should* do and what they *actually* do, and efforts toward greater training and dissemination of effective treatments are being made to bridge this gap. In line with these efforts, the goal of this book is to provide a practical "how to" guide that synthesizes research, offers clear explanations of the theoretical underpinnings of CBT with specific intervention techniques, illustrated by case examples, and addresses critical topics to boost favorable outcomes.

Understanding Anxiety

The terms *fear*, the normative response to immediate perceived threat (Marks, 1969), and *anxiety*, which occurs in response to anticipated or future threat (Johnson & Melamed, 1979), are often used interchangeably in current vernacular, and we will do so as well. These experiences are universal and, at times, even beneficial. From an evolutionary perspective, fear and anxiety are adaptive. They serve a safety function, alerting us to potential dangers and motivating us to escape or avoid threatening situations. In daily life, anxiety can enhance performance, such as a student being motivated by anxiety to study for a test. Thus, anxiety is a necessary part of life because, without it, we would succumb to innumerable dangers or underperformance.

While a certain degree of anxiety is normative and beneficial, some individuals develop anxiety disorders, which are characterized by excessive or difficult to control levels of anxiety. That is, they perceive more risk in a given situation than actually is justified. Some individuals also experience anxiety in situations that are objectively safe. This unwarranted and excessive anxiety can become problematic by impeding or interrupting daily activities, social interactions, and/or educational or occupational functioning, resulting in significant functional impairment.

Anxiety Disorders

Our current categorical classification system, the *Diagnostic and Statistical Manual of Mental Disorders, Fifth Edition* (DSM-5; American Psychiatric Association, 2013), gives the impression that there are discrete and distinct anxiety disorders. These diagnoses, however, are primarily differentiated based on the stimuli that elicit the fear response. There is considerable overlap among the disorders in that they all are based on an excessive, maladaptive fear response including overestimation of threat, physiological reactivity, and behavioral avoidance of anxiety-provoking stimuli. Moreover, the high rates of comorbidity among anxiety disorders and the fact that treatment for all anxiety disorders is similar, regardless of specific diagnosis, underscore the commonalities. As such, we, like others (e.g., Lebowitz & Omer, 2013), advocate for viewing anxiety disorders as a collective. Still, accurately diagnosing symptoms lays the foundation for providing proper education to children, their parents, and other caregivers.

The DSM-5 includes 11 anxiety disorder diagnoses. All diagnoses require that symptoms: (1) cause clinically significant interference in functioning, (2) are not better accounted for by another mental health disorder or medical condition, and (3) are not the result of a substance. Specific diagnostic criteria and clinical features of the most relevant ones among youth are briefly provided here.

Separation Anxiety Disorder

A) At least three of the following:
   a. Excessive distress upon actual or anticipated separation from attachment figure.
   b. Persistent worry about losing or harm befalling attachment figure.
   c. Persistent worry about experiencing an event that would result in separation (e.g., being kidnapped or getting lost).
   d. Reluctance or refusal to go places because of fear of separation.
   e. Fear or avoidance of being alone or places without attachment figure.
   f. Refusal to sleep away from home or without being near attachment figure.
   g. Repeated nightmares with separation themes.
   h. Physical symptoms such as headache or nausea when faced with actual or anticipated separation.
B) Symptom duration of at least four weeks, commonly longer than six months

While most common in childhood, separation anxiety disorder (SAD) can persist into or emerge during adolescence or even adulthood. SAD is defined by excessive fear or anxiety triggered by separation from an attachment figure such as a parent. Common features include excessive worry about harm coming to attachment figures (e.g., illness, dying) or events occurring that would result in separation (e.g., being lost or kidnapped). Behaviorally, children with SAD may avoid (i.e., demonstrate significant reluctance or refusal) separation from their attachment figures. They may physically block their parents from leaving (e.g., the young child who holds on to his mother's leg as she tries to leave the house or the teenage girl who stands behind her parents' car to prevent them from backing out of the garage). When separation is unavoidable, children with SAD may make efforts to stay connected through repeated phone calls or texts. Bedtime is particularly challenging for many children with SAD, and they may refuse to sleep alone or want to fall asleep before parents do. These children experience significant distress and somatic symptoms such as headaches and nausea, and they may cry or tantrum when faced with actual or anticipated separation. The level of fear exceeds what is developmentally normative, and symptoms may manifest somewhat differently over time (e.g., emergence of more cognitive-based symptoms as children age).

Selective Mutism

A) Failure to speak in certain situations (e.g., school) despite speaking in others.
B) Interference in academic or occupational achievement or social communication.
C) Symptom duration of at least one month (not limited to first month of school).
D) Failure to speak despite knowledge of and comfort with the expected language.

Children with selective mutism (SM) possess the ability to speak but are unable or unwilling to do so in some circumstances, most commonly speaking freely at home but not elsewhere. The lack of speech is typically not associated with a communication disorder. Rather, it appears to be a variant of social anxiety or, perhaps, a fear of one's own voice. There is variability in the degree of mutism that may be exhibited. For example, some children with SM may speak, either in a whisper or full volume, with peers at school but not teachers while others may interact only nonverbally (e.g., smiling, pointing, nodding head) with peers and teachers while still others may appear almost nonresponsive when anyone, including parents, attempt to engage them outside of the home. Some children with SM will speak to their parents in public or at school, while others fail to produce any sort of speech outside of their home. Parents are often surprised when first informed about their child's lack of speech, describing their children as "chatterboxes" at home. While most frequently SM symptoms remit by adulthood, it can persist for decades, especially if left untreated.

Specific Phobia

A) Significant fear related to a specific object or situation.
B) Contact with phobic object consistently elicits anxiety.
C) Phobic object is avoided or endured with significant distress.
D) Fear is out of proportion to actual danger.

E) Symptoms are persistent, usually with at least six months duration.

F) Specify: animal, natural environment, situational, blood-injection-injury, other.

A specific phobia is characterized by extreme and excessive fear triggered by a specific object or situation. Common phobias include: animals (e.g., insects, spiders, snakes, dogs), natural environment (e.g., storms, heights, water), blood-injection-injury (e.g., needles, medical procedures), situations (e.g., enclosed spaces, elevators, flying), choking, vomiting, costumed characters (e.g., clowns or mascots), and dentists/doctors. It is also quite common for individuals to have several co-occurring specific phobias. Individuals with phobias actively avoid the feared object or endure with great distress if avoidance is not possible. Other behavioral manifestations of fear may include tantrums, particularly in younger children, freezing, and crying. While some can identify cognitive content related to their feared object (e.g., a bee will sting, and it will hurt), others simply experience a strong emotional response (i.e., fear and urge to avoid). Individuals may have panic attacks when faced with the feared object. The fear and resulting avoidance must cross the threshold of clinically significant impairment in functioning to warrant a diagnosis. That is, if, despite significant fear, functioning is not negatively impacted, then diagnostic criteria are not met (e.g., a child who is scared of snakes but does not regularly encounter related stimuli). Some children may realize that their fear is unreasonable or excessive, but this insight is not required for a diagnosis.

Social Anxiety Disorder

A) Significant anxiety in at least one social situation that involves potential scrutiny from others.

B) Fear that behavior or signs of anxiety will result in negative evaluation from others.

C) Anxiety is almost always provoked by these social situations.

D) Anxiety-provoking situations are avoided or endured with significant distress.

E) Anxiety is disproportionate to the situation.

F) Symptoms are persistent, typically with at least six months duration.

The hallmark of social anxiety disorder (SOC) is a fear of negative evaluation by others. Socially anxious youth are afraid of being judged, embarrassed, or humiliated by their peers and/or adults. These social fears can be triggered by informal social situations, such as meeting new people or having conversations, as well as performance-based/evaluative situations, such as reading aloud in front of the class. Other commonly feared social situations include: participating in class, extending social invitations, talking on the phone, eating in public, using public restrooms, being photographed, musical or athletic performances, taking tests, being assertive, and dating. Individuals with SOC may experience anticipatory anxiety prior to entering a social situation as well as during and/or following the situation. Maladaptive cognitions (e.g., "They'll think I'm dumb/weird," "They won't like me") and physical symptoms of anxiety, including panic attacks, are common. Many socially anxious youth worry about others noticing and judging their anxiety symptoms (e.g., blushing, sweating, shaking), and this worry exacerbates physical symptoms, leading to a self-fulfilling cycle. There also may be social skills deficits (i.e., lack of skill or inability to produce skill when appropriate) that result in negative feedback from others, in turn increasing their anxiety. They may isolate themselves or avoid social interactions or activities due to anxiety, not a lack of interest in socializing (Brown, Silvia, Myin-Germeys, & Kwapil, 2007; Coplan, Prakash, O'Neil, & Armer, 2004).

Generalized Anxiety Disorder

A) Excessive worry about a number of topics occurring more days than not, persisting for at least six months.
B) Worry is difficult to control.
C) Associated with at least one (three for adults) of the following:
   a. Restlessness
   b. Easily fatigued
   c. Concentration difficulties
   d. Irritability
   e. Muscle tension
   f. Sleep disturbance

Youth with generalized anxiety disorder (GAD) experience excessive worry about routine topics, such as school, social or interpersonal issues, the future, world events, their or significant others' health, performance, perfectionism, day-to-day tasks and activities, and family issues like parental divorce or finances. Children with GAD often seek excessive reassurance, which provides, at most, temporary reprieve from anxiety because their worries persist. Their worries are hard to control, and many children report being unable to "turn their brains off" at night and experiencing disrupted sleep. Unfortunately, being tired can make it even more difficult to manage anxiety and can have a deleterious effect on concentration and academic performance. This can create a vicious cycle, particularly for children who worry about school performance.

Obsessive Compulsive Disorder

While obsessive compulsive disorder (OCD) has been separated into a different diagnostic category in the DSM-5, we have opted to include it because the treatment of OCD is similar to other anxiety disorders in terms of conceptualization and intervention.

A) Presence of obsessions and/or compulsions.
B) Obsessions and compulsions take up at least one hour per day and/or cause significant impairment in functioning.

OCD is a heterogeneous disorder that is often misdiagnosed. Nicknamed the doubting disease, it is characterized by an intolerance of uncertainty. Like GAD, OCD is a worry-based disorder. In contrast, however, obsessive worries tend to concentrate on a specific theme, may have seemingly unusual or atypical content, and do not respond to logic or reasoning. Obsessions are defined as illogical, intrusive, unwanted, and recurrent thoughts, images, impulses, or rigidly adhered to rules. Common obsessions include contamination (e.g., fear of germs), harm (e.g., fear of hurting oneself, fear of house fires), symmetry (e.g., need to even out), scrupulosity (e.g., fear of offending a deity), superstitious fears, hypochondriasis/health fears, and numbers (e.g., odd numbers are bad). Obsessions typically boil down to either a fear of something bad happening or "just right" (i.e., no feared outcome, violating the obsessive rule just feels wrong). Obsessions are distressing or anxiety-provoking and are accompanied by compulsions, which are overt or mental actions designed to reduce distress, prevent feared outcomes from occurring, or get rid of unwanted thoughts. Common compulsions include: excessive or ritualized hand washing, checking, evening out, praying, asking repeated questions, doing actions a certain number of times, and following specific routines, restarting if messed up. There is a functional relationship between obsessions and compulsions in that obsessions increase anxiety while compulsions serve to decrease it.

Prevalence

Anxiety disorders are widely known as the most common psychiatric condition. In fact, they are more common in youth than depression or externalizing disorders (Cartwright-Hatton, McNicol, & Doubleday, 2006; Essau, Conradt, & Petermann, 2000). Actual prevalence rates, however, vary widely, depending on research methodological factors such as representativeness of study samples, specific disorders assessed, inclusion of functional impairment criteria, time frame covered, and mode of assessment and informant(s) used to derive diagnoses (e.g., standardized diagnostic interviews, self-report measures, child and/or parent report). Lifetime prevalence rates of anxiety disorders are estimated at around 30 percent (e.g., Merikangas et al., 2010; Ormel et al., 2015). When specific requirements regarding severity and negative impact on daily functioning are included, prevalence rates drop to 5 to 10 percent (e.g., Ormel et al., 2015; Polanczyk, Salum, Sugaya, Caye, & Rohde, 2015; Vicente et al., 2012). Most anxiety disorders emerge during childhood or adolescence, with some typically presenting earlier in life than others, and the rates increasing steadily with age (e.g., Costello & Angold, 1995; Essau et al., 2000; Ormel et al., 2015). SOC is the most prevalent anxiety disorder across the life span (Ballenger et al., 1998). In childhood, however, SAD is the most common (Cartwright-Hatton et al., 2006) while panic disorder and SM are relatively rare (APA, 2013). Across most diagnoses, females are more likely to meet criteria than males, typically at a 2:1 ratio (APA, 2013; Merikangas et al., 2010; Ormel et al., 2015); the exception, however, is OCD, which is more common in males during childhood and then becomes more prevalent in females into adulthood (Geller et al., 1998; Last & Strauss, 1989). Extensive research also demonstrates high comorbidity rates within anxiety disorders and with depressive disorders, externalizing disorders, and sleep-related problems (e.g., Essau et al., 2000; Kendall, Brady, & Verduin, 2001; Last, Strauss, & Francis, 1987; Peterman, Carper, & Kendall, 2015).

Etiology

Despite advances in science, we still do not have a definitive answer to the common question, "What causes a child to develop an anxiety disorder?" Ample empirical and anecdotal data indicate that anxiety disorders run in families (Last, Hersen, Kazdin, Orvaschel, & Perrin, 1991; Turner, Beidel, & Costello, 1987). The mechanism(s) by which anxiety disorders are transmitted, however, is not fully clear. Several factors appear to make a causal contribution. Complicating the picture further, interactions among these factors seem to be evident. For example, environmental elements may impact whether a genotype is expressed, or genes may moderate the effect that an environment has on a child. Simply put, there appear to be several etiological pathways that involve a combination of nature and nurture.

Biological Etiological Pathways

Biological contributions to the etiology of anxiety disorders include genetic, neurobiological, and physiological influences. At least 30 percent of the risk in the development of an anxiety disorder is accounted for by inherited genes (Beidel & Alfano, 2011; Gordon & Hen, 2004; Skre, Onstad, Turgersen, Lygren, & Kringlen, 2000), yet the weight of this contribution is believed to vary depending on the specific disorder (e.g., specific phobia appears to have a higher genetic influence than SAD or SOC; Eley, Rijsdijk, Perrin, O'Connor, & Bolton, 2008). Beidel and Alfano (2011) concluded that children inherit a propensity toward developing an anxiety disorder in general, termed *anxiety proneness*, which may be manifested in a number of ways including those described below.

Anxiety disorders are considered neurobiological conditions associated with differences in the anatomical structures and/or the functions of structures in the brain and nervous system. These differences are be-lieved to contribute to the onset of anxiety disorders, though causality has not been sufficiently demonstrated, perhaps in part due to research and technology limitations. Extant correlational studies have found sig-nificant differences in the neuroanatomy of children with and without anxiety disorders, with anxiety disorders being associated with larger vol-umes of the amygdala (Qin et al., 2014), superior temporal gyrus (De Bellis et al., 2002), and thalamus (Gilbert et al., 2000) and lower volume of the white matter of the dorsolateral prefrontal cortex and anterior cin-gulate (Lazaro et al., 2014), although findings have not been consistently replicated. Overactivity of the amygdala, frontal cortex, hippocampus, and thalamus also has received substantial attention (Guyer et al., 2008; Sweeney & Pine, 2004). Neurotransmitters, the chemical messengers in the brain, may also play a role in the development of anxiety disorders, specifically serotonin, dopamine, and norepinephrine (Sweeney & Pine, 2004). These neurotransmitters modulate neural circuitry and are impli-cated in the conditioning and expression of fear responses.

Several studies also have shown that the offspring of anxious adults have higher physiological reactivity than those of nonanxious adults, regardless of whether the children have been diagnosed with an anxiety disorder (Grillon, Dierker, & Merikangas, 1997; Grillon, Dierker, & Merikangas, 1998; Turner, Beidel, & Roberson-Nay, 2005), suggesting that differences in physiological responses may be implicated in the de-velopment of anxiety disorders. Moreover, converging data from rhesus monkeys, human infants and youth, and socially anxious adults suggest that anxiety disorders may be associated with a pattern of physiological reactivity in heart rate variability (i.e., whether heart rate decreases over the course of stressful tasks, which is indicative of habituation) that is dif-ferent from their nonanxious counterparts (Moehler et al., 2006; Monk et al., 2001; Suomi, 1986; Turner, Beidel, & Larkin, 1986). It also has been suggested that physiological overarousal paired with less ability to ef-ficiently regulate may lead to an anxiety disorder (Suveg & Zeman, 2004).

Temperament, defined as "a relatively stable pattern of behavioral tendencies that emerges early in life" (Sweeney & Pine, 2004, p. 40), has been implicated in the development of anxiety disorders. Behavioral inhibition (BI), a specific temperament style characterized by distress in and avoidance of novel situations, is of particular interest. Young children with BI display a pattern of physiological reactivity that is different (Kagan, Reznick, & Snidman, 1987). BI in early childhood has been linked to later social anxiety (Biederman et al., 2001; Hayward, Killen, Kraemer, & Taylor, 1998) but not to other anxiety presentations such as specific phobias or SAD (e.g., Schwartz, Snidman, & Kagan, 1999). Some children obviously outgrow BI, so to speak, because the correlation between BI and later SOC is not 100 percent, and there appear to be notable physiological reactivity differences between those who do and do not develop psychopathology. Parenting style likely moderates this relationship (e.g., Rubin, Hastings, Stewart, Henderson, & Chen, 1997; Park, Belsky, Putnam, & Crnic, 1997), highlighting the complex interactions between biological and environmental influences.

Environmental Pathways

Environmental and experiential contributions to anxiety are evident and may represent other ways in which anxiety disorders are transmitted from parents to children. Parental modeling and reinforcement, or more broadly parenting style, may contribute to the development of anxiety disorders. Individual learning experiences may as well. The most direct illustration of learned fear is classical conditioning. In their classic study of Little Albert, Watson and Rayner (1920) paired a loud noise, which naturally elicits a fear response in toddlers, with the presence of a white rat, which did not naturally frighten Albert. With repeated pairings, he began to exhibit fear when presented with the rat, even in the absence of a loud noise, and this fear generalized to other white furry things. While clearly some individuals with anxiety disorders can trace the onset of symptoms to a specific conditioning or triggering event, most cannot (King, Eleonora, & Ollendick, 1998). Furthermore, not everyone who experiences a potentially conditioning event goes on to develop an anxiety disorder (di Nardo et al., 1988; Rachman, 1990).

Operant conditioning is another learning process that seems to play a large role in the maintenance and exacerbation of anxiety symptoms. In a nutshell, operant conditioning theory holds that the consequence of a behavior will either reinforce or punish it, subsequently increasing or decreasing, respectively, the likelihood that behavior will occur again. Positive reinforcement is the addition of something desirable while negative reinforcement removes something aversive. With regard to anxiety disorders, the experience of anxiety is quite aversive. Thus, responses that alleviate it will be negatively reinforced. For example, a teen with contamination fears who experiences relief after washing her hands will be more likely to wash again in the future. Over time, the relief will last for shorter intervals, and the hand washing becomes increasingly problematic. Mowrer (1947) proposed a two-factor theory of learning in which fear is initially classically conditioned, then behavioral avoidance is reinforced via operant conditioning.

Observational or vicarious learning may also play a role in the development of anxiety disorders and is especially pertinent when considering treatment for anxious youth. Parental modeling of anxiety, including openly expressing their own fears, encouraging avoidance, and making certain types of verbalizations toward their child (e.g., cautionary instructions), is associated with higher anxiety in children (e.g., Barrett, Rapee, Dadds, & Ryan, 1996; de Rosnay, Cooper, Tsigaras, & Murray, 2006; Gerull & Rapee, 2002; McFarlane, 1987; Muris, Steerneman, Merckelbach, & Meesters, 1996). While it is logical to assume that an overprotective parenting style would have a causal effect on childhood anxiety disorders, the direction of causality remains complex and is being further investigated. For example, Lebowitz and Omer (2013) conceptualize childhood anxiety disorders as interpersonal problems that exist within the parent–child relationship: a child has difficulty regulating emotional responses, parental distress increases, and the parent intervenes to regulate for the child. This pattern prevents the child from learning how to self-regulate and contributes to avoidance of triggers by both the parent and the child.

Conclusion

Anxiety disorders are the most prevalent psychiatric disorders among youth. These neurobiological conditions are characterized by maladaptive fear responses leading to behavioral avoidance. The etiology of these disorders is multifaceted, believed to include a combination of biological and environmental influences.

CHAPTER 2

Evaluation and Assessment

Evidence-based assessment of childhood anxiety is fundamental to inform accurate diagnostic impressions and treatment planning. It also sets the stage to monitor the child's gains and response to treatment over time.

Normative versus Clinical Anxiety

In order to ascertain whether a child's anxiety warrants intervention, it is first important to understand the normative features and typical sequence of fears among youth. Indeed, fear responses are considered part of the natural developmental trajectory and necessary for children to learn boundaries to promote their safety in the world. The experience of fear also prepares children to navigate life's challenges. Similarly, certain ritualistic behavior is considered normative and adaptive for younger children. Routines, such as those at bedtime, provide an increased sense of self-efficacy and predictability in an environment that is perceived as out of control (Evans, Gray, & Leckman, 1999).

Extensive research has examined typical fears across specific age groups (e.g., Ollendick, Matson, & Helsel, 1985). Results demonstrate that normative fears change across ages and stages of development and tend to be mild and transitory (Ollendick, King, & Muris, 2002). Furthermore, the general experience of fear is believed to peak around age 7 years, with females reporting higher fear than males across age groups (Laing, Fernyhough, Turner, & Freeston, 2009; Ollendick, Yule, & Ollier, 1991).

For very young children around age 1 to 2 years, common fears include separation from a caregiver, toileting activities, and physical injury. Among 3- to 5-year-olds, fears of animals, the dark, and imaginary creatures are most common, while young school-age children show greater school-related anxiety as well as fears of storms, death, and physical safety.

For preadolescent and adolescent youth, fears focus most on test taking, social interactions, and performances. Table 2.1 provides a summary of the common fears at each age group (Ollendick et al., 1985).

The challenge for parents, educators, and professionals is to determine when a fear exceeds normative development and becomes dysfunctional. Several factors can be considered to aid in this determination. Perhaps the most important factor is the degree of interference in social, emotional, academic, or physical functioning. Anxiety can lead to isolation, poor self-concept, social skills deficits, poor academic achievement, and numerous physical complaints. With physical symptoms, it is especially common for anxious children to complain of headaches and gastrointestinal symptoms. They may also have sleep difficulties, which in turn affect their daytime functioning and lead to further physical symptoms and concentration difficulties. Other factors to consider when differentiating between normative and clinical levels of anxiety include how excessive the fear is for the situation, how difficult it is for the child to calm down

Table 2.1 *Normative fears across age groups*

Age	Fears
Infancy	Loss of physical support Loud noises
1–2 years	Separation from caregiver Strangers Toileting activities Physical injury Heights
3–5 years	Animals Imaginary creatures Dark Being alone
6–9 years	Storms School Death Personal safety
10–12 years	Tests Personal health
13 years and older	Social interactions and events Economic and political concerns

despite being provided logical evidence and explanations against the fear, how persistent the fearful reaction remains over time, how appropriate the fear is for the child's age or developmental stage, and how significant the child's avoidance or other dysfunctional coping strategies become.

Assessment Procedures

To determine the presence and severity of anxiety, a comprehensive assessment that consists of a multimethod and multi-informant approach offers the greatest benefits. Additionally, the inclusion of assessment methods and instruments that have been empirically tested and demonstrated to have good psychometric properties is advised. Methods most often include structured diagnostic interviews, questionnaires, and functional analysis (King, Muris, & Ollendick, 2005).

Clinical Interview

Most clinicians begin an assessment with a general interview to gather an overview of the history and current circumstances from the child and parents' points of view. Specific domains often included in this interview are developmental and medical history, academic history, peer relations, an account of psychosocial stressors, and home situation and family relations. McConaughy (2013) offers a helpful and thorough resource on conducting clinical interviews with youth and parents.

While there are benefits of a clinical interview, there also are noteworthy limitations. Benefits include the ability to interact with the youth and parents in a more informal and conversational manner, which can foster rapport building and allow for observations of their interaction style. It also can "set the stage" for and encourage openness during the more structured and symptom-focused portion of the assessment. Reliance on a clinical interview, however, is discouraged, as it can produce considerable error due to interviewer bias. It also limits the clinician's ability to fully ascertain and identify possible comorbid conditions. The following structured interviews and rating scales are recommended to surmount these limitations.

Structured Diagnostic Interviews

The most widely used diagnostic interview for childhood anxiety has been the *Anxiety Disorders Interview Schedule for DSM-IV: Child and Parent Versions* (ADIS-C/P; Silverman & Albano, 1996). At this time, there is not an updated version for DSM-5; however, the ADIS-C/P remains a gold standard for assessing the full spectrum of anxiety-related problem behaviors and diagnoses in youth, including school refusal behavior, separation anxiety, social phobia, specific phobia, panic disorder, agoraphobia, obsessive compulsive disorder, and posttraumatic stress disorder. It also allows for assessment and differential diagnosis of mood and externalizing disorders as well as screenings of substance abuse, psychosis, selective mutism, eating disorders, somatoform disorders, and specific developmental and learning disorders. The ADIS-C/P includes two semi-structured interview schedules, with one designed for the child as informant and a second for the parent. Strong psychometric properties for the ADIS-C/P are established (e.g., Silverman, Saavedra, & Pina, 2001).

A shorter structured diagnostic interview designed to assess DSM-5 and ICD-10 psychiatric disorders for children ages 6 to 18 years is the *Mini International Neuropsychiatric Interview for Children and Adolescents* (MINI-KID; Sheehan et al., 2010). It was designed as a concise yet comprehensive interview, which offers the benefit of a shorter administration time (i.e., 15 to 50 minutes) compared to many diagnostic interviews. It can be administered to the parent and child together or separately, and there is also a parent-only version available. The MINI-KID includes assessment of all anxiety and related disorders as well as screenings across diagnostic categories, including mood, substance use, eating, psychotic, externalizing, tic, and pervasive development disorders. It also offers a well-validated suicide module.

For assessment of OCD symptoms in youth, the *Children's Yale-Brown Obsessive Compulsive Scale* (CY-BOCS; Scahill et al., 1997) is considered the standard semi-structured clinician-administered assessment. It consists of a detailed symptom checklist of common obsessions and compulsions as well as a 10-item rating scale to assess OCD symptom severity in the past week. On the severity scale, each item is rated on a 0- to 4-point Likert scale, yielding a total severity score (range 0–40). The severity score offers a helpful guide when considering treatment recommendations (e.g., intensity of treatment services) and monitoring the youth's progress over time.

Rating Scales

Paper-and-pencil rating scales offer an additional and relatively easy format for assessment. Because several questionnaires map onto DSM diagnostic categories and include clinical norms, they also can assist with differential diagnosis and monitoring progress over time. The following is a summary of several commonly used rating scales.

The *Spence Children's Anxiety Scale* (SCAS; Spence, 1998; Spence, Barrett, & Turner, 2003) was developed to correspond broadly to the DSM-IV diagnostic dimensions for youth anxiety disorders. Several versions are available, including child and parent versions validated for use with 7- to 18-year-olds as well as preschool versions for parents and teachers of children aged 2.5- to 6.5-years old. Each version yields a total score and subscale scores to reflect obsessive compulsive symptoms, generalized anxiety, separation anxiety, social anxiety, panic/agoraphobia, and fears of physical injury. The scales have good psychometric properties (e.g., Spence et al., 2003) and are available in the public domain.

The *Screen for Child Anxiety Related Emotional Disorders* (SCARED; Birmaher et al., 1999) is a 41-item youth and parent report instrument that also is available in the public domain. Raters endorse each item (e.g., "I worry/My child worries about sleeping alone") on a 3-point Likert scale from 0 (*not true/hardly ever true*) to 2 (*very true/often true*). The SCARED includes five subscales that measure generalized anxiety, separation anxiety, social phobia, school phobia, and physical symptoms of anxiety, as well as a total score, with higher scores indicating more anxiety. The subscales and total score have sufficient reliability and validity for use with youth ranging from 8 to 18 years old (Birmaher et al., 1999).

For rating scales designed to assess OCD symptoms, the *Children's Obsessive Compulsive Inventory-Revised* (ChOCI-R; Uher, Heyman, Turner, & Shafran, 2008) is a 32-item measure comprised of 20 questions that evaluate the presence of specific obsessions and compulsions and 12 questions that assess severity of OCD symptoms and associated impairment. Youth and parent versions are available, with both demonstrating good internal consistency as well as convergent and discriminant validity. The *Children's Florida Obsessive Compulsive Inventory* (C-FOCI; Storch et al., 2009) also offers a brief youth report of OCD symptoms. The C-FOCI consists of a 17-item symptom checklist and a 5-item severity scale, suitable for comparison with the CY-BOCS. The inventory has demonstrated adequate internal consistency and convergent and discriminant validity.

Family Variables

Growing research also encourages the inclusion of assessment procedures examining familial variables due to their significant relation to children's symptom severity and treatment response. For example, although not entirely consistent, several studies have demonstrated the direct relation between higher parental psychopathology and poorer youth anxiety treatment outcome (e.g., Cobham, Dadds, & Spence, 1998; Southam-Gerow, Kendall, & Weersing, 2001). Another familial variable that has received increasing attention is the level of family accommodations (FAs) made for the child's anxiety disorder. FA involves parent behaviors that are aimed at reducing the disorder-related distress experienced by the child and has been shown to have a deleterious impact on the course of the child's anxiety condition (Storch et al., 2015). These findings highlight the importance of assessing familial variables to improve treatment outcomes in anxious youth.

Several rating scales are available to assess these familial variables. For parental psychopathology, the *Depression, Anxiety, and Stress Scales* (DASS; Lovibond & Lovibond, 1995) offers a brief adult self-report instrument to assess negative emotional states of depression, anxiety, and tension/stress. There is the full 42-item instrument and a shorter version that consists of 21 items. Both versions have established psychometric properties (Antony, Bieling, Cox, Enns, & Swinson, 1998). Examples of brief screening questionnaires that can be employed to assess anxiety symptoms in adults include the *Generalized Anxiety Disorder 7-item scale* (Spitzer, Kroenke, Williams, & Lowe, 2006) and the *Penn State Worry Questionnaire* (Meyer, Miller, Metzger, & Borkovec, 1990).

To assess FA across anxiety conditions, the *Family Accommodation Scale—Anxiety* (FASA; Lebowitz et al., 2013) is the most frequently used rating scale. It consists of a 13-item rating scale that assesses the frequency of parent participation in child symptoms, modification of schedules and routines, parental distress relating to the level of accommodation, and child responses when accommodation is not offered. Child and parent versions are available. The FASA has good internal consistency as well as convergent and divergent validity (Lebowitz et al., 2013). For assessment of FA specific to OCD, the *Family Accommodation Scale for Obsessive Compulsive Disorder—Self-Rated Version* (FAS-SR; Pinto, Van Noppen, & Calvocoressi, 2013) offers a 19-item parent rating scale to measure the degree to which family members facilitate or participate in youth's OCD rituals and/or avoidance. This measure also has established internal consistency and convergent validity.

Functional Behavioral Analysis

An additional assessment procedure that is especially relevant as it pertains to treatment planning is a functional analysis. Through behavioral observations and/or daily logs, clinicians, parents, teachers, and even youth can record antecedents of the child's anxiety, specific behavior that occurs with anxiety, and consequences that follow such behavior. This information can be synthesized with other methods of assessment to aid in differential diagnosis and identification of factors that maintain the child's anxiety. Daily logs can offer a relatively simple way to gather this information to elucidate patterns of anxiety, as well as fluctuations in the child's behavior across contexts. When used over time, it also can offer information on adherence and response to treatment procedures. Key components to include in daily logs may be the triggering situation (i.e., antecedent), the child's behaviors, physical and cognitive experiences (in the case of youth's self-monitoring), and what occurred following this behavior (i.e., consequence). In the book *Modular Cognitive Behavioral Therapy for Childhood Anxiety Disorders,* Chorpita (2006) offers helpful examples of observation logs that can be used for this purpose.

Conclusion

Evidence-based assessment can significantly enhance outcomes for anxious youth. In terms of best practices, it is suggested that clinicians utilize structured diagnostic interviews, which provide structure while allowing for use of clinical judgment. Rating scales from multiple informants, including the child or adolescent as well as caregiver(s), provide additional and important perspectives on the youth's symptoms. It is also critical to assess the potential for associated problems, including FAs and parent psychopathology, which can affect treatment response. Finally, a solid functional analysis and ongoing monitoring of treatment progress (using child and caregiver reports) are key to informing the intervention, assessing the child's response, and adjusting the plan where appropriate.

CHAPTER 3

Treatment Overview

Following in the footsteps of medicine, there has been a push within the field of psychology for evidence-based practice (EBP; Spring & Altman, 2005), with the aims of reducing error in clinical decision-making and promoting the implementation of beneficial treatments by integrating research, clinical judgment, and individual patient values/characteristics (Society of Clinical Child and Adolescent Psychology, 2012). Integral to EBP is the consideration of and preferential reliance on empirically supported treatments, which are those that have demonstrated efficacy in research studies and clinical trials (Chambless & Hollon, 1998). Over the past several decades, a robust evidence base has been established with two clear treatment options for pediatric anxiety disorders: cognitive behavioral therapy (CBT) and medication. It should be noted that there is minimal empirical support for biofeedback, play therapy, rational emotive therapy, and psychodynamic therapy (Chorpita et al., 2011), and no support for Eye Movement Desensitization and Reprocessing (EMDR), client-centered therapy, or primarily listening-based therapy (Higa-McMillan, Francis, Rith-Najarian, & Chorpita, 2016).

Review of the Current Evidence Base

Cognitive Behavioral Therapy

CBT is a specific therapy modality based on a clear theoretical conceptualization. While there are numerous published treatment manuals available to guide clinicians (e.g., *Coping CAT*, *Social Effectiveness Therapy for Children*, *Modular Cognitive-Behavioral Therapy for Childhood Anxiety Disorders*), the prototypical elements of CBT for anxiety disorders will be addressed in detail in subsequent chapters. As a therapeutic approach,

CBT is goal oriented and solution focused, with interventions designed to reduce current symptoms, improve functioning, and prevent future relapses, rather than discover the origin of symptoms or develop insight. Another hallmark of CBT is the use of between session homework assignments, which is critical for supporting skill acquisition and implementation. CBT is short-term, averaging 12 to 15 sessions (Silverman, Pina, & Viswesveran, 2008) with content that builds sequentially. Though the content of individual sessions may vary by protocol, they tend to be structured, with a typical agenda being homework review, introduction of new education or skill, practice, and assignment of new homework. The course of a standard CBT protocol is: assessment, psychoeducation, skill building (e.g., relaxation training, cognitive restructuring, problem-solving, social skills training) and/or graduated exposure and response prevention, and relapse prevention (e.g., Albano & Kendall, 2002). Commonly, contingency management and/or self-reward is also included to promote motivation and adherence (Keeton & Ginsburg, 2008; Silverman et al., 2008).

The first clinical trials examining the efficacy of CBT for childhood anxiety disorders were published in the 1990s (e.g., *Coping CAT*; Kendall, 1994). Since that time, abundant research support has been garnered, with converging results from individual treatment studies as well as meta-analyses, indicating that CBT is efficacious, typically yielding large effect sizes (e.g., Chorpita et al., 2011; In-Albon, & Schneider, 2006; Ollendick & King, 1998; Silverman et al., 2008). Extending beyond efficacy research, which occurs in controlled settings and often with exclusion criteria that may not mimic real-world clinical settings, numerous studies have also demonstrated the effectiveness of CBT in community settings (Baer & Garland, 2005; Ginsburg & Drake, 2002; Masia, Klein, Storch, & Corda, 2001). Not only has CBT been shown to produce positive results at the conclusion of active treatment (typically 12 weeks), results have also shown that gains are maintained for extended periods, even several years (Beidel, Turner, Young, & Paulson, 2005; Kendall & Southam-Gerow, 1996; Kendall, Safford, Flannery-Schroeder, & Webb, 2004; Piacentini et al., 2014). CBT outcomes appear to be durable across a range of ages, ethnicities, formats, and settings. For example, comparable effects have been found for both individual and group formats (Flannery-Schroeder & Kendall, 2000; Silverman et al., 2008). Variants have also modified levels of parental/family involvement (Barrett, 1998; Silverman et al., 1999; Wood, Piacentini, Southern-Gerow, Chu, & Sigman, 2006).

Medication

Medication has also been established as an efficacious treatment for childhood anxiety, with the selective serotonin reuptake inhibitors (SSRIs) gaining clear status as the preferred pharmacological intervention because of their ability to reduce symptoms while being generally well tolerated (e.g., Rynn et al., 2011). Numerous research trials demonstrated that SSRIs consistently outperform placebo for a number of anxiety disorders and OCD with moderate effect sizes (March et al., 1998; McGuire et al., 2015; Strawn, Welge, Wehry, Keeshin, & Rynn, 2015). Tricyclic antidepressants and serotonin-norepinephrine reuptake inhibitors (SNRIs) have also yielded symptom reduction, though these medications have less empirical support. Moreover, they have higher side-effect profiles and require more structured medical monitoring to ensure that weight, vital signs, cholesterol, and cardiac functioning are not negatively impacted (e.g., Rynn et al., 2011; Strawn et al., 2015). Medications affecting the glutamatergic, GABAergic, or adrenergic systems such as memantine, D-cycloserine, riluzole, and propranolol may have some potential for treating anxiety disorders (Rynn et al., 2011). Available data, however, are preliminary at best, and the safety and utility in children are not yet known.

SSRIs appear to be safe, though longitudinal data are lacking, and the impact of medication use during critical developmental periods is not fully understood. They are also fairly well tolerated, with few side effects and no need for ongoing laboratory monitoring (Rynn et al., 2011). Typical side effects include nausea, headache, and drowsiness, and activation (which presents like hyperactivity or agitation) may be seen in some youth. Side effects often dissipate within one to two weeks or can be lessened by a "starting low and going slow" titration schedule. SSRIs do carry a black box warning that their use may cause increased suicidality in youth, which has caused concern for some parents and providers.

This warning was issued based on a meta-analysis in which the risk for suicidality (defined as suicidal behavior or ideation) for depressed teens treated with SSRI medication was higher than for those on placebo (risk ratio = 1.66) (Hammad, Laughren, & Racoosin, 2006). Since then, however, many authors have argued that the risk of *not* using SSRIs is greater as suicide attempts and completions increased in the mid-2000s following the issuance of the warning and subsequent decline in use of SSRIs. It is important to note that increased risk for suicidality has not been found for anxious youth (Henry, Kisicki, & Varley, 2012; Strawn et al., 2015). Overall, in many cases, the benefits of SSRIs outweigh the risks (Garland, Kutcher, Virani, & Elbe, 2016).

Combined CBT + Medication

Ample research has compared CBT or medication to wait-list control conditions, and both have demonstrated efficacy, with effect sizes typically being larger for CBT than medication in meta-analyses (e.g., Abramowitz, Whiteside, & Deacon, 2005; McGuire et al., 2015). It is only recently, however, that these two monotherapies were compared in head-to-head trials. Two large-scale, multisite clinical trials, the Child/Adolescent Anxiety Multimodal Study (CAMS) and the Pediatric OCD Treatment Study (POTS), compared CBT to SSRI (sertraline) and compared both independent treatments to combined treatment (CBT+SSRI) and placebo for youth with anxiety disorders and OCD, respectively. Results from CAMS indicated that CBT and sertraline are both better than placebo but not significantly different from each other, and their combination achieved the best results (Walkup et al., 2008). Results from POTS found that combined treatment (CBT+SSRI) and CBT alone yielded the strongest remission rates (POTS, 2004).

Treatment Moderators

Unfortunately, not all anxious youth respond favorably to treatment. In fact, treatment outcome studies usually indicate that around 60 percent respond (e.g., Barrett, 1998; Beidel, Turner, & Morris, 2000; Kendall, 1994; Silverman et al., 1999), leaving a considerable minority with suboptimal responses. More recent, and certainly future, research efforts have focused on identifying predictors and moderators of treatment outcome, which may shed light on important decisions, such as which treatment may be best for whom. Patient demographics such as ethnicity and gender do not seem to affect response to treatment (e.g., Compton et al., 2014), whereas baseline symptom severity may predict poorer response to CBT (Southam-Gerow et al., 2001). Youth with more severe symptoms may warrant longer treatment duration, higher intensity of treatment, different sequencing of interventions, or something else altogether (Compton et al., 2014). The impact of comorbidity on response to anxiety treatment is not quite clear; sometimes the presence of other conditions does not appear to affect anxiety treatment (Kendall et al., 2001; Rapee, 2003), while it may in other cases (Berman, Weems, Silverman, & Kurtines, 2000).

The impact of parental anxiety or other psychopathology on treatment outcomes has been of interest. To address this question, Cobham et al. (1998) compared group CBT (GCBT) and GCBT including parental anxiety management (GCBT + PAM). They found greater improvement for the GCBT + PAM for youth with anxious parents but no difference between groups for children with nonanxious parents; these results suggest that addressing parental anxiety may facilitate treatment response for their children, though these authors noted that research methodology could have contributed to their findings. Interestingly and counter to predictions, Gonzalez et al. (2015) found that higher levels of parental anxiety predicted a faster and more positive response to sertraline treatment, though it did not impact response to CBT.

Making Clinical Decisions

There are numerous considerations when deciding whether to treat anxious youth via CBT, medication, or a combination. CBT is a safe and efficacious first-line intervention, particularly for mild to moderate symptoms, while combined CBT + SSRI is ideal for severe symptoms or significant functional impairment. Medication may be opted for initially under certain circumstances such as lack of access to CBT or the presence of significant comorbid depression that warrants more immediate intervention. Other considerations that may tip the balance toward medication over CBT include past experiences with therapy, family's attitude toward therapy as well as their expectations of change, and motivation for therapy (Henry et al., 2012) (Table 3.1).

While combined treatment may provide the most benefit, the sequencing of treatments may be important. The current evidence base, however, does not provide clear guidance on this issue, necessitating the use of clinical judgment. If a child is not responding as expected after 8 to 12 weeks of CBT, augmenting with a medication may be beneficial (Rynn et al., 2011). In contrast, treating first with medication may provide some relief and allow for more engagement in CBT (Bernstein et al., 2000; Keeton & Ginsburg, 2008), though it is possible that patients may then attribute changes to the medication rather than themselves, which could limit learning effects and coping when medicine is discontinued. Moreover, starting medication first may dampen motivation to learn and utilize anxiety management skills, increasing risk of future relapse (Keeton & Ginsburg, 2008). Simultaneous initiation of CBT and medication may be best under certain conditions such as: comorbid anxiety and depression, the presence of parental psychopathology, and/or a history of

Table 3.1 *Comparing pros and cons of treatment options*

	Advantages	**Disadvantages**
Medication	+ Consistently superior to placebo + Moderate reduction in symptoms + Maintenance of gains with continued treatment	− Side effects − Relapse upon discontinuation
CBT	+ Consistently superior to placebox + Significant reduction in symptoms + Typically more effective than medication alone + Maintenance of gains following conclusion of treatment + No side effects	− Lack of access to CBT providers − Requires higher degree of motivation − More time and effort intensive

Bottom Line: *Expert consensus guidelines, based in large part on available data as well as clinical judgment from leaders in the field, deem CBT as first-line intervention for pediatric anxiety disorders and OCD if symptoms are mild to moderate and combined CBT + SSRI medication if symptoms are severe or result in significant functional impairment.**

* Agency for Healthcare Research and Quality, 2012; AACAP, 2007; Davis, May, & Whiting, 2011; March, Frances, Carpenter, & Kahn, n.d.; Rynn et al., 2011

unsuccessful treatment. Despite positive effects for CBT and/or medication, a significant proportion of anxious youth remain symptomatic. As such, augmenting with additional therapeutic interventions is often necessary and, realistically, occurs in clinical practice. Potential augmenting strategies include: increasing the intensity or dose of treatment(s), incorporating parent training or treatment of parental anxiety, and addressing comorbidities or treatment interfering behaviors (e.g., adherence).

Conclusion

EBP is a model of clinical decision-making that relies on empirical data and clinical judgment while taking into account individual characteristics. At this time, CBT, SSRI medication, and their combination are the most effective and appropriate interventions for pediatric anxiety disorders and OCD.

CHAPTER 4

Understanding the Cognitive Behavioral Model

Theoretical Underpinnings and Rationale for Treatment

The cognitive behavioral model has broad applications, informing the conceptualization of and guiding treatment for numerous psychiatric and medical presentations including depressive disorders, eating disorders, chronic pain, psychotic disorders, functional gastrointestinal disorders, substance abuse disorders, etc. With regard to anxiety disorders, CBT is based on conceptualizing anxiety as a tripartite construct comprised of three interconnected components: physiological arousal, cognitive processes, and behaviors (Lang, 1968). These components interact in reciprocal fashion, resulting in the subjective experience of anxiety. The basis of treatment is that intervening in one area will impact the others as well.

Physiological Arousal (Feelings)

When anxiety is triggered, the sympathetic nervous system, a branch of the autonomic nervous system commonly referred to as the "fight or flight (or freeze)" response, is activated. Physiological changes can include: increased heart rate, shortness of breath or difficulty breathing, shakiness, numbness or tingling sensations, dry mouth, lump in the throat or choking sensations, increased blood pressure, hot or cold sensations, nausea or stomach distress, urge to void bladder or bowels, lightheaded or faintness, sweating, and visual changes (e.g., tunnel vision, seeing spots). A sudden rush of physical signals can occur during panic attacks. Other forms of anxiety may be associated with physical signals such as muscle tension, headaches, and gastrointestinal distress; the latter two are particularly common in anxious children. While anxiety always includes some physical signal(s) or physiological arousal, the saliency of those signals may vary by specific disorder or by child. That is, not every anxious child will experience the same physiological reactivity or have the same somatic complaints, but more complaints are associated with overall anxiety severity (Ginsburg, Riddle, & Davies, 2006).

Cognition

The cognitive component of anxiety encompasses attentional and executive functioning features as well as the content and patterns of thoughts and beliefs. Regarding the former, tests of attentional biases have consistently demonstrated that anxious individuals attend more to threat cues (Williams, Matthews, & MacLeod, 1996; Salum et al., 2013), which may make them more susceptible to anxiety. These attentional biases may affect how information is processed, encoded, and remembered. Moreover, Muris and Field (2008) posit that anxious youth have interpretation biases in that they attach more threatening meaning to neutral stimuli or require less information to perceive danger compared to their nonanxious counterparts. They may also display memory biases, at least with emotionally laden memories, that contribute to anxiety.

Perhaps of more interest from a treatment standpoint are maladaptive and distorted automatic thoughts (ATs) and core beliefs. Thoughts that arise automatically and often without awareness initially in any given situation are referred to as ATs. Core beliefs, on the other hand, are more deeply held beliefs about the self and others that govern an individual's approach to life and serve as a filter through which experiences and events are interpreted. For example, two teens who fail a math test may interpret this event very differently based on their beliefs. Teen A has a core belief that she is smart and capable. Her ATs when she receives the poor grade may be "That was a really hard test. If I study harder next time, I'll do better." Teen B adheres to the faulty belief that she is stupid. Her ATs upon seeing the failing grade may be "I'm never going to get this. I'm going to fail out of high school, and I'll never get into college."

The content of and extent to which maladaptive cognitions play a role in a child's experience of anxiety may vary depending on specific anxiety disorder presentation (e.g., less prominent in specific phobias), age, and cognitive development. That is, very young children lack metacognitive abilities, meaning they may not be aware of their internal self-talk (Flavell, Flavell, & Green, 2001). With cognitive maturity, older youth are able to consider more abstract concepts.

Behavior

The behavioral component consists of actions, either overt or mental, that children do or, more importantly, do not do when anxious. Anxious children avoid or escape anxiety-provoking situations. Upon doing so, anxiety is alleviated, and avoidance is negatively reinforced. Over time, this pattern results in worsening anxiety because the child never has the opportunity to learn that discomfort will abate with the passage of time alone, and corrective information to refute maladaptive cognitions is never obtained. Behavioral avoidance includes the measures by which a child avoids or reduces distress or discomfort or prevents feared outcomes from occurring. Avoidance can occur on a clear, obviously observable level, for example, by refusing to go to anxiety-provoking places, as well as in subtler ways such as averting gaze or saying "I don't know" to avoid answering a question incorrectly in class. Other behaviors associated with anxiety in youth can include crying, clinging to caregiver, stuttering, reassurance-seeking, and rituals or routines. Some anxious children also exhibit noncompliant or oppositional behaviors when anxious (Beidel & Alfano, 2011).

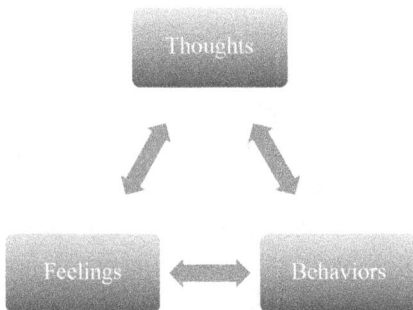

CBT is based on the aforementioned conceptualization and aims to target each of the three components via a number of strategies. Of note, the crux of treatment involves modifying the behavioral component in order to facilitate changes and improvements across thoughts and feelings. A major reason for this focus is due to the very nature of these components. While we cannot directly control how we think and feel, we can control what we do. Because thoughts, feelings, and behaviors are interconnected, helping children to take charge and learn to use adaptive and effective coping strategies in place of anxious-avoidant behaviors improves all three components.

Teaching Children the Cognitive Behavioral Model and Orienting to Treatment

There is a myriad of ways to introduce children to CBT for anxiety, limited only by creativity! We use a number of metaphors to illustrate principles based on a child's developmental level, interests, and symptoms. A common and favorite example is the description of a smoke detector as a metaphor for anxiety. Children have learned that homes are equipped with smoke detectors, which have the important job of sensing smoke, an indicator of fire, and sounding an alarm to alert us to take the necessary steps to ensure safety, such as leaving the house and calling 911. Most of the time, the presence of these devices is all but forgotten. Imagine, though, what it would be like if that smoke detector started going off every time you lit a candle, used the stove, or for no apparent reason. What would you do? Would you continue to run out of the house and call 911? Hopefully not. You would figure out that these are false alarms and respond accordingly—maybe by fanning the air in front of the alarm, opening a window, or simply ignoring the alarm until it stops. Anxiety is like our body's built-in smoke detector. When it works the way it is supposed to, anxiety keeps us safe by alerting us to potential threats, motivating us to act quickly and effectively to avoid or escape danger, and preventing us from engaging in harmful behaviors. As such, anxiety is natural, necessary, and helpful. Some people's anxiety systems, however, are "too good" at their jobs. These individuals experience anxiety signals when they are not in danger or in excess of what a situation warrants. For these individuals, anxiety interferes with functioning, which constitutes an anxiety disorder.

Another common strategy in working with youth is externalization, which involves personifying the anxiety as a separate entity from the child, often giving it a name (e.g., Freeman et al., 2014). Some youth may decide to give their anxiety a silly name, like Mr. Worry or the Brain Bully (or, some personal favorites: Mr. Stinky Feet, Veruse Lola, the worry bug, and the chattering monster); others, particularly teens, may opt to call it simply "Anxiety" or "OCD." Externalizing anxiety can make it easier for a child to recognize anxious thoughts as distinct from their own and encourage more rational or helpful ways of thinking. Moreover, externalizing can also be helpful for engagement in exposures, as discussed in a later chapter. In this framework, children learn to be "brave and bossy" in response to their anxiety. Some children resonate with viewing their anxiety as a bully or adversary. Alternatively, other children may find it more helpful to think of anxiety as a helper-gone-awry who needs to be trained or recalibrated. Movies such as *Inside Out* have helped some children readily identify with externalizations of emotions, including the "Fear" character.

Conclusion

Anxiety is comprised of three interrelated components: thoughts, physical sensations, and behaviors. Maladaptations in any or all of these can fuel the subjective experience of anxiety. While CBT aims to target all components, the primary driving force for change is through the behavioral component because it focuses on the child's response to anxious thoughts and feelings. Children are taught adaptive coping strategies to use in place of anxious-avoidant reactions. Through this process, children become empowered and learn how to "retrain their alarm" to work for them rather than against them.

CHAPTER 5

Relaxation Training

As described in the previous chapter, the experience of physical tension and somatic symptoms is a chief component of anxiety disorders. Physical symptoms may result from worry and anxiety, such as when a child with SAD develops a stomachache in anticipation of being away from his parent. These symptoms also can contribute to or exacerbate the severity of worry and anxiety. Therefore, teaching children relaxation strategies to reduce and manage the physical component is an important conduit to interrupt the cycle of anxiety and promote anxiety management. This chapter presents a variety of relaxation and mindfulness-based strategies that help to reduce physical tension and enhance children's stress and anxiety management.

Diaphragm Breathing

Diaphragm breathing, also known as belly breathing, activates the parasympathetic nervous system, inducing a calming effect that can be especially beneficial when a child's manifestation of anxiety includes shaking, crying, shortness of breath, gastrointestinal distress, and/or dizziness. It also can be easily and discretely applied across settings. We often describe it to children as their "secret weapon" that they can use any time without others being aware of it.

When introducing the concept, it is most helpful to include information that is relevant to that particular child's symptoms and interests. For example, if a child experiences stomach pain or headache as a manifestation of anxiety, it can be helpful to emphasize how diaphragm breathing both relaxes the body and helps the brain to release natural pain-fighting chemicals like endorphins and enkephalins that reduce pain and discomfort. If a child is interested in sports, it may be helpful to underscore how diaphragm breathing is incorporated in top athlete training to enhance their stress management and endurance.

The importance of regular practice should be emphasized. Use the child's personal experiences with practicing a sport or musical instrument to help them understand how practice when they are not anxious will help them use this tool when they are anxious.

> *Therapist:* "I understand you play baseball, is that right?"
> *Child:* "Yeah, I've been playing for a few years."
> *Therapist:* "How does your coach help you get ready for games?"
> *Child:* "Well, he definitely has us practice a lot. We practice every-thing over and over again."
> *Therapist:* "Wow, that's a lot of hard work, and I bet it helps on game day. We actually can think about practicing the breathing exer-cise in the same way . . . if you didn't practice baseball before the games, how do you think it would turn out?"
> *Child:* "Probably not so well. We just wouldn't be as prepared."
> *Therapist:* "That's right, and when anxiety pops up, we also want to be sure you're prepared. We know that practicing the belly breathing twice a day right now will help you get better at it and be ready to use it."
> *Child:* "Yeah, that makes sense."

To encourage the child's motivation to practice, it often is helpful to work with parents on establishing an incentive plan. When starting out, we encourage children and parents to focus on practicing during calm times for the first two weeks to strengthen their ability to use the tool effectively. Following this, the child is encouraged to continue formal practices in addi-tion to active application of the tool. To further encourage application, it is important to help the child identify their common physical cues or "warn-ing signs" of anxiety. This can help them learn when to apply this tool.

When introducing diaphragm breathing, explain to the child that the goal is to help them learn to take slow, deep breaths through the belly. It can be helpful to explain how babies—and even dogs!—naturally breathe through their belly, and as we get older our breath shifts up to the chest, which results in shallow breathing and further activation of the "fight or flight" response when we become stressed or anxious. The following general script can be used to teach diaphragm breathing:

> *Lean back and get into a comfortable position. Place one palm on your chest and one on your belly. Take a deep breath and notice which hand moves more (typically the child will notice the chest moving). Now, breathe slowly in through your nose and imagine that the air is going down a long tube that takes it into your belly. As you breathe the air in, it blows up a balloon in your belly, making it expand. As you breathe out slowly, the balloon deflates and your belly goes back down. Continue with slow steady breaths . . . counting to yourself 1, 2, 3 as you breathe in, and slowing down even further as you breathe out 1, 2, 3, 4, 5 . . .*

Various descriptors and adjustments can be incorporated to encourage the child's active and effective participation. For example, children can be directed to make a "slow leaky tire" sound to slow down the exhalation and fully "deflate" before breathing in again. This can be turned into a fun competition with parents to see who can be the *slowest* leaky tire (i.e., exhale the longest). With this exercise, the goal is to expel all of the air possible, which results in the body automatically taking in a deep, cleansing breath. The use of bubbles can be a fun interactive activity when teaching younger children. They can be encouraged to breathe out slowly in order to form a larger bubble. Many children also find it fun to practice lying down and seeing if they can lift an object (e.g., stuffed animal, small book) placed on their belly through the movement of air alone. There are numerous formats for youth to practice and apply diaphragm breathing. See Table 5.1 for additional examples of breathing exercises.

Visual Imagery

Visual imagery engages a child's imagination to help bring on a state of calmness or relaxation. Essentially, children are taught to visualize a calm or relaxing place, either real or imagined. The more salient the imagery, the more effective this tool can be. That is, incorporating not just visual input but also imagining other sensory information can be helpful for making the imagery more robust. While there are countless guided imagery exercises available, the

Table 5.1 Examples of diaphragm breathing exercises

Name of exercise	Description for youth
Square Breathing	Breathe in to a count of 4, hold for a count of 4, breathe out to a count of 4, hold for a count of 4, repeat. The child can draw a square in the air as they practice.
Hot Cocoa Breathing	Imagine holding a yummy cup of hot cocoa. Deeply breathe in the aroma of the chocolate. Blow out slowly to cool it in preparation for drinking. Repeat four times.
Name Breathing	Using the letters in your name, focus on one letter at a time as you breathe out.
Breathing Buddy	Place a soft toy on the belly. While breathing, notice the gentle rising and falling of the toy.
Birthday Candles Breathing	Imagine your fingers on one hand are birthday candles. Take a slow breath in while you raise each finger, counting silently 1, 2, 3, 4, 5. As you exhale, slowly blow out the "candles" counting each finger as it lowers one at a time, until your hand becomes a fist. As you breathe in the next breath, the candles reappear. Repeat.

change your channel technique (Anderson, Smith, & Christophersen, 2011) is one that is portable and developmentally appropriate for even young children (3+ years). In this exercise, the mind is compared to a TV that has different channels, and the child is in charge of the remote control. When a channel is changed, the scene completely changes. Children are instructed to "change their channel" from a worry or scary scene to a calm or relaxing one. Caregivers can coach the child through changing their channel until mastery occurs. Young children may also benefit from using a photograph to help aid their imagery practice by making the scene more real.

> *Therapist:* "Let's practice changing your channel."
> *Child:* "OK."
> *Therapist:* "Close your eyes. Now, change your channel. Imagine something calm and relaxing . . . I want to go to the same channel you are, but I'll need your help to get there. Where are you?"
> *Child:* "In the clouds."
> *Therapist:* "What do you see?"
> *Child:* "I see white puffy clouds all around me."
> *Therapist:* "Good. What else can you see?"
> *Child:* "The sky is blue. There's a bird flying by over there."

Therapist: "What sounds can you hear?"

Child: "I hear the bird chirping. The wind is also making a little rustling sound."

Therapist: "What do you smell?"

Child: "It smells like cotton candy here."

Therapist: "What do you taste?"

Child: "I don't really taste anything in my special place."

Therapist: What can you feel on your skin?"

Child: "It's warm, like the sun is shining on me. The clouds are fluffy and soft, kind of like cotton balls. I can feel the breeze, too."

Therapist: "Great job changing your channel!"

Progressive Muscle Relaxation

Progressive muscle relaxation is another form of relaxation that targets muscle tension and tightness that intensify with stress and anxiety. While adult versions of this exercise tend to take 20 to 30 minutes, shorter (i.e., 5 to 15 minutes) versions are recommended for children to better match their attention spans. It also is valuable to incorporate visual imagery and/ or an interactive component depending on the child's developmental stage. A classic script that was written by Koeppen (1974) for young children instructs them to imagine being a turtle and to "pull your head into your shell," and to imagine holding a lemon in each hand and to "squeeze all the juice out." Ollendick and Cerny (1981) also provide an adapted script for teaching muscle relaxation to slightly older children. It is helpful to provide an audio recording of the exercise for use at home. Other shorter exercises that are especially fun for younger children include the "Robot/Ragdoll" and the "Spaghetti Test"; both involve tightening all muscles of the body for 10 to 15 seconds (i.e., like a robot or dry spaghetti noodle) and then loosening the muscles and going limp like a ragdoll or cooked noodle.

Mindfulness

There is a growing body of research demonstrating the benefits of mindfulness for promoting emotion regulation and reducing the physiology of stress and anxiety among youth. Mindfulness refers to living in the present moment and observing thoughts, feelings, and sensations that arise moment to moment in an open, nonjudgmental, and nonreactive manner (e.g., Kabat-Zinn, 1994). Mindfulness fosters cognitive control, prosocial behavior, compassion/empathy, stress reduction, and self-regulation (Hölzel et al., 2011; Marcus et al., 2003). Because research specifically examining the benefits of mindfulness for youth has yielded similar outcomes (Schonert-Reichl et al., 2015; Zoogman, Goldberg, Hoyt, & Miller, 2014), there is a growing movement to bring mindfulness into child anxiety treatment and even into K-12 education.

Mindfulness helps children learn to pause for a moment, to bring purposeful attention to their experiences, and to cultivate a sense of kindness and compassion toward themselves and others. As with other calming strategies, it is helpful to take a lighthearted and playful approach when teaching mindfulness to youth. In her book *Sitting Still Like a Frog*, Snel (2013) provides a plethora of mindfulness exercises for youth and caretakers to enjoy. To encourage nonjudgmental observation, Snel offers various "open-minded observation" exercises that can be modified based on the child's age. These exercises help children bring attention to their experiences while also teaching them to separate out their awareness of thoughts from (mis)interpretations (i.e., anxious or negative judgments about self and/or others in the experience). These exercises also foster concentration, retention of details, and, with practice, less prominent and disruptive interpretations.

One "open-minded observation" exercise involves showing the child a tray of twelve items, covering the tray with a cloth after 30 seconds and then instructing the child to describe or write down what they can recall. With repeated practices (e.g., three times weekly for two weeks), children remember more items and retain more details about the items. This exercise offers an opportunity to demonstrate how observation without judgment enhances concentration and confidence. Another exercise for older children involves finding a twig and having them draw it on paper. They are instructed to draw exactly what they see and not what they think they see. After repeating this for a few days in a row, they can see more and more of the twig, and the drawing becomes more accurate. This exercise similarly reinforces the power of observation and awareness. See Table 5.2 for additional examples of mindfulness exercises adapted for youth.

Table 5.2 Examples of mindfulness exercises

Name of exercise	Description for youth
Mindful Eating	Slow down the process of eating a snack by noticing each sensation one by one; notice how it feels, smells, and then tastes by taking a very slow bite. Then chew slowly and notice every sensation as you swallow it.
Your Personal Weather Report (Snel, 2013)	Pause and check in with your emotional and physical feelings. What is the weather like inside you? Is it sunny, cloudy, or is there a storm brewing? Stay close to this feeling for a while, and notice that your personal weather report changes on its own over time, just like the weather outside.
"Spidey" Senses (Jazwierski, 2013)	Superheroes, like Spiderman, have superpower senses to help them be aware. Switch on your super "Spidey senses" to find out what you can taste, smell, hear, see, and feel in this moment.
Mindful Bubbles	Imagine bubbles floating up in front of you. Now place each thought and sensation inside a unique bubble, one by one, floating up and away.
Thought Leaves (Willard, 2010)	Imagine thoughts forming as autumn leaves that land softly on an empty and accepting blanket.
Slow Race	Walk as slowly as possible without stopping movement. Notice that you have to focus all of your attention on walking, or you lose your balance!

Relaxation at Bedtime

For many children, bedtime can prove to be a time fraught with higher anxiety and stress. This may be due to specific nighttime fears, such as darkness and separation from parents, or due to worries and preoccupations that disrupt the mind. If this occurs, it is especially important to establish a bedtime routine that integrates active use of relaxation and mindfulness exercises to promote a quiet mind and sleep. A helpful bedtime routine can include the following: (a) a specified time to turn off all electronics, ideally at least an hour before bedtime; (b) a specified time to start the bedtime routine; (c) a relaxation or mindfulness exercise during the routine, which may be a guided audio exercise; and (d) a "bedtime basket" of quiet activities for the child to use after parents say goodnight. The basket can be especially beneficial for use with children who have trouble separating and/or falling asleep. Parents can redirect the child to use these items at bedtime to encourage self-soothing. Children often enjoy helping parents decide which items to include in their basket. Common ideas include a book, a coloring book and colored pencils, a special stuffed animal, a word search, quiet music or nature sounds, family photos, a school yearbook, coping cards that offer helpful coping thoughts and ideas for pleasant visualizations (e.g., a favorite vacation, something to look forward to), and a small flashlight for the activities. Incorporating a reward system to encourage the child's adherence to the bedtime routine also can be important to its success.

Conclusion

Relaxation strategies offer youth the opportunity to learn more about the physiological effects of anxiety and to gain confidence and skills in their management of these symptoms. Similarly, mindfulness encourages an objective awareness and acceptance of anxious thoughts and sensations, and, in turn, a greater ability to center oneself in the face of anxiety. These skills are integral to the child's anxiety "toolkit" and provide a foundation for other, more active tools, including exposures.

CHAPTER 6

Cognitive Techniques

Cognitive interventions target the maladaptive thoughts that drive anxiety either by changing the content of the thoughts or by reducing an individual's reactivity to them. This chapter focuses on three main types of cognitive techniques: cognitive restructuring, defusion or distancing, and coping thoughts. Before discussing these techniques, however, it is important to understand and recognize cognitive distortions.

Cognitive Distortions

Certain problematic thinking patterns are associated with anxiety disorders. These automatic thoughts, worries, predictions, and beliefs are irrational and often characterized by logical fallacies or distortions, also known as thinking errors or "brain tricks." Think of the way your reflection gets warped when you look in a fun house mirror, or imagine putting on a pair of tinted glasses; everything you see is now filtered through that lens, distorting the color. Cognitive distortions are the fun house mirrors and the tinted lenses. Most anxious thoughts boil down to an overestimation of threat and an underestimation of one's ability to cope: "Something bad is going to happen, and I can't handle it." Extensive descriptions of cognitive distortions have been published elsewhere (e.g., Burns, 1980; Clark & Beck, 2010; Grayson, 2003), but some of the most common ones are included in Table 6.1.

Youth can learn to identify their thoughts and recognize distortions, but developmental adaptions must be made. One way to do so is to rely on externalization, separating the voice of anxiety from the child. "What does OCD tell you will happen?" or "What is Mr. Worry saying about going to that sleepover?" Another way to use externalization is to personify specific cognitive distortions (e.g., "Arya Sure" to embody intolerance of

Table 6.1 Common cognitive distortions

Distortion or error
All-or-none thinking (also called black or white and dichotomous thinking) Thinking in extreme, either/or terms. *I have to get an A or I'm a failure.*
Mind reading (core distortion in SOC) Assuming someone else's thoughts, judgments, or perceptions, typically in a negative or critical manner. *He thinks I sound dumb.*
Catastrophizing Exaggerating the likelihood of something bad happening or how bad it will be, blowing things out of proportion, jumping to the worst-case scenario. *Mom is late. She must have gotten into a car accident and died.*
Fortune telling Predicting negative outcomes for future events. *No one at my new school is going to like me.*
Perfectionism Unrealistically high standards, rigidly held views of right and wrong, often associated with "shoulds." *I should never make a mistake in school.*
Discounting the positives Dismissing positive attributes and overly emphasizing the negative, qualifying positives with a negative, "yeah but." *She's just saying that to be nice. She's nice to everyone.*
Intolerance of anxiety Belief that anxiety will last forever and that you must get rid of it, belief that you cannot handle or tolerate the discomfort.
Intolerance of uncertainty (core distortion of OCD) Excessive doubt or distress in the absence of 100% certainty. *Am I sure I unplugged the hair dryer?*
Labeling Essentially calling yourself a name or applying a negative label. *I'm such an idiot!*

uncertainty). Children can also come up with their own brain trick characters. One older elementary school-aged girl created "Kenny Do it Dude" to reflect her dominating maladaptive thought: "I can't do it" (underestimation of coping ability/intolerance of anxiety). Another middle schooler was very into Harry Potter, magic, and fairy tales. She externalized her anxiety, named "The Villain," and we created the Villain's Spell Book to illustrate cognitive distortions; "spells" included the Zebra Charm (black or white thinking) and Disappearing Act (makes the positives disappear/discounting the positives). Other strategies for helping children and teens recognize cognitive distortions include teaching them to recognize "code words" that signal distortions such as "what if," "yeah but," or "should."

Cognitive Restructuring

Cognitive restructuring refers to the process of identifying and modifying maladaptive or irrational automatic thoughts and core beliefs and replacing with rational ones. There are four steps in basic cognitive restructuring: identifying thoughts, labeling thinking errors or distortions, evaluating both the accuracy and helpfulness of these thoughts, and generating a rational response. Key questions can be helpful for evaluating anxious thoughts (Table 6.2). They are designed to help determine whether thoughts are accurate (i.e., rational, factual) and helpful. Responses to key questions can be summarized to generate a rational response. Rational responses must be believable and refute the original anxious thought. Simply replacing a negative thought with a positive one is inadequate and ineffective as it often does not satisfy those two requirements. For example, challenging the anxious thought "Someone is going to break into my house" with "No one will break in" is not as effective as "The chances of someone breaking into my house are very small. It has never happened before. I live in a safe neighborhood, and my mom locks the door at night."

Table 6.2 Sample key questions

Where is the proof/evidence for this thought? Against?
What happened last time?
What are the chances that will happen?
How bad would that be? Could you handle it?
Will it be a big deal in a week? Month? Year?
What's another way to look at the situation?
What's another explanation?
What would you tell a friend?
So what if . . . ?

There are numerous ways to introduce the concept of cognitive restructuring to children. Perhaps one of our all-time favorites is the "stepping in poo" metaphor, shared by Phillip Kendall in a training years ago.

Imagine I'm walking along when all of a sudden I step in a pile of dog poo. I think, 'Oh no! What if I get to work, and everyone thinks I stink, but I took a shower! What if it ruins my shoes? I love these shoes!' How am I feeling? Anxious. Now, imagine I'm walking along and step in a pile of dog poo, and I think, 'This is just my luck. I deserve this.

Today is going to be awful.' How am I feeling? Sad. Now, I'm walking along and step in the poo. This time I think 'That stupid person! They shouldn't be allowed to have a dog!' I'm feeling angry. Finally, I'm walking along, step in the poo and think, 'That stinks. Oh well, no big deal.' How am I feeling now? I stepped in poo either way it goes, and no one likes to step in poo. I had four very different reactions, though. Why? Because what I said to myself was different. Which one is correct? Trick question . . . none of them are necessarily right or wrong, but the last one is certainly more helpful. We're going to learn how to think in helpful ways when 'poo' happens.

There are a variety of methods for practicing cognitive restructuring with youth. For example, the idea of bossing back worries, hinging on the externalization of anxiety, is helpful for many children. We often practice bossing back worries via role-play. Children are instructed to "win the argument." Caregivers then verbalize the child's worries, and the child "bosses it back" either by making refuting statements or asking key questions. Other children have found "Thought Detective" or the idea of taking thoughts to court interesting. In this framework, youth are taught to look for clues or evidence to challenge their anxiety. The book *Helping Your Anxious Child* (Rapee, Spence, Cobham, & Wignall, 2000) offers a downloadable form for parents to use with children that involves the detective approach. Another activity for younger children is squashing worries. Have the child write a worry on a piece of foam (or paper), and spread the pieces on the floor. The child jumps onto a worry, "squashing it," while simultaneously stating a rational response. Another strategy to counter discounting the positive thoughts is the use of "but at least." Youth are taught to catch "yeah, buts" and follow up with a "but at least . . . ." For example, "I didn't get a part in the play . . . but at least I was brave enough to try out for it!"

A note to caregivers: one pitfall to avoid is doing the cognitive restructuring for the child. That is, the more you try to talk a child out of negative thoughts, the more they talk themselves into them. Your job is to guide the child to arrive at the rational responses. Ask key questions to help the child evaluate the accuracy and helpfulness of their thoughts, but refrain from supplying the answers and efforts to convince the child out of the anxious or negative thought.

Distancing or Defusion

The goal of distancing or defusion is to help the youth disengage from anxious thoughts. Rather than suppressing anxious thoughts, which does not work, or arguing with anxious thoughts (see cognitive restructuring), which also is not always effective, particularly when targeting illogical or intrusive thoughts characteristic of OCD, distancing aims to help the youth take a mental step back, so to speak, acknowledge the thought, then move on. Doing so helps reduce reactivity to thoughts. Said another way, it takes the power away from thoughts. Essentially, youth are taught to label anxious or obsessive thoughts, without engaging in the content. When an anxious thought arises, they may think "That's OCD. It doesn't mean anything!" or "That's a brain trick! I'm not falling for it." More examples of cognitive distancing training can be found in Wagner (2003; 2013) and March and Mulle (1998). Another defusion technique involves repeating the anxious thought until it loses meaning and, therefore, emotional reactivity. Huebner (2008) uses the metaphor of "chewing" on a thought like a piece of gum—it eventually loses it flavor! To introduce to a child, try an experiment of repeating a word over and over for one minute. Usually before the time is up, the child will smile or laugh. Use this as an opportunity to prompt for observations.

> *Therapist:* "What happened? What's so funny?"
> *Child:* "It sounds like gibberish, and I'm getting tongue tied."
> *Therapist:* "Exactly! When you say it over and over, it loses meaning and starts to seem silly. The same thing will happen with a scary thought. It may just take a little longer. Are you willing to try it out?"

Coping Thoughts

While the content of anxious and maladaptive thoughts varies across individuals and disorders, almost all include an underestimation of one's ability to cope. Coping thoughts are designed to help bolster youths' confidence in their ability to cope with anxiety and manage challenging situations, as opposed to targeting the actual content of anxious thoughts. Coping thoughts can also help youth reinforce themselves for being brave, using skills, or successfully navigating challenges. Basically, coping thoughts are the inner cheerleader or coach. Generating coping thoughts together can be helpful for anxious children. Ensuring access to these coping thoughts during times of anxiety is also important. For example, creating a coping card (an index card that has coping statements written on it or an electronic card or note on a cell phone) that children can read when anxious can be helpful. Table 6.3 provides examples of coping thoughts.

Table 6.3 Sample coping thoughts

Just because I think it, it doesn't make it true!	It's never as bad as it seems.
Practice will make it better and easier!	I can do this!
I am brave!	I'm in charge, not anxiety!
I can boss it back!	It will get easier with time!

Conclusion

All cognitive interventions target thought processes associated with anxiety. Three main interventions are cognitive restructuring, distancing and defusion, and coping thoughts. Cognitive restructuring involves identifying and changing anxious thoughts and beliefs, developing more rational and helpful ways of thinking. Distancing and defusion techniques serve to change the relationship with and reaction to anxious thoughts and beliefs, helping the youth to observe thoughts with greater objectivity. Finally, coping thoughts help bolster a child's self-efficacy in managing anxiety effectively.

CHAPTER 7

Behavioral Techniques

Exposure with Response Prevention

Exposure therapy is considered the primary and most active component of CBT for anxiety across age groups (Beidel et al., 2000; Kendall et al., 2005). While evidence-based treatment integrates additional techniques, such as cognitive restructuring and relaxation strategies, it is through the exposure process that corrective learning, increased tolerance, and habituation (i.e., "getting used to" triggers) truly take place. Despite its proven effectiveness, many clinicians are tentative to apply this technique with children. They experience their own fear and concerns with children's ability to handle facing their fears. As aptly stated by Abramowitz, Deacon, and Whiteside (2011, p. 299), "clinicians often enter the mental health field with the desire to *reduce*, as opposed to *produce*, distress." Unfortunately, this hesitation prevents children from gaining a primary component of treatment that has repeatedly been shown to yield long-term improvements in anxiety management and relief (Hofmann & Smits, 2008; Kendall, Hudson, Gosch, Flannery-Schroeder, & Suveg, 2008). As a result, there is a growing initiative to promote better dissemination of and trainings in the use of exposure therapy with youth.

Introducing Exposure Therapy

Exposure involves the process of purposely facing a fear in order to gain tolerance and corrective information to overcome the fear and pattern of avoidance. At a very basic level, it means doing the opposite of what anxious thoughts and feelings are leading us to do. Children may view their anxiety as "bad" and something they must "get rid of" and avoid. When introducing the concept, it is important to explain the nature of anxiety and its adaptive function in our lives. As described in Chapter 6, the metaphor of anxiety as the body's natural alarm system is often employed and recommended (e.g., Chorpita, 2006). In addition to the "smoke detector" metaphor, the example of a dog phobia can be utilized because nearly all youth are familiar with this fear, even when they do not have a personal experience with it. Specifically, children are encouraged to consider what the specific fear or worry is for those who are afraid of dogs (i.e., being attacked or bitten) and whether this is a true alarm or a false alarm. For children who lack this fear, this is an especially helpful example because they can quickly identify this as a false alarm. It also underscores how avoidance strengthens fear and prevents corrective information to overcome the fear and rectify the alarm's response.

Another favorite story to orient children to exposures is the "standing double back flip" analogy described in the following dialogue:

> *Therapist:* "Did I ever tell you I was on the gymnastics team when I was in high school?"
>
> *Child:* "No."
>
> *Therapist:* "I was and, in fact, I can still do a standing double back flip! I can even do it in my office if I move some of the furniture out of the way. Do you believe me?"
>
> *Child:* Looks skeptical. "I don't know."
>
> *Therapist:* "You look uncertain. What makes you think I can't do one?"
>
> *Child:* Giggling, "Well, most grown-ups can't do a flip."
>
> *Therapist:* "Well, I've been practicing for 20 years, and I'm really good at it. Convinced?"
>
> *Child:* "Not exactly. There's not enough room in here."
>
> *Therapist:* "I do have to move the furniture around, but there's plenty of room. I tuck into an itty bitty ball to flip. Convinced?"
>
> *Child:* "Not really."
>
> *Therapist:* "What would it take to convince you?"
>
> *Child:* "Prove it!"
>
> *Therapist:* "For the record, I can't and never could do a standing double back flip. You did a nice job thinking it through then ultimately saying, 'prove it,' which is exactly what we're going to do with your anxiety."

Types of Exposures

There are three types of exposures, congruent with the three components of anxiety (e.g., Abramowitz et al., 2011). The determination of the types of exposures to include in a treatment plan is made based on the symptom profile of the individual. *In vivo* exposures involve confrontation of specific, real-life anxiety triggers. Examples include having a child with a dog phobia spend time with dogs and having a teen with contamination-focused OCD touch door handles without washing. Imaginal exposures involve facing intrusive thoughts, images, and feared imagined scenarios. These may be incorporated to amplify the experience of *in vivo* exposures or used on their own to target the feared "worst-case scenarios." For example, a child with a vomit phobia and school refusal may have intrusive thoughts and images about another child vomiting in front of them in the classroom or cafeteria. An imaginal exposure involves having the child develop a vivid story about their fear coming true. Through repetitive practice of the imaginal exposure, the child can increasingly manage the thoughts and images, leading to less anxiety and greater confidence and tolerance when these thoughts are present. Interoceptive exposure is the third type of exposure. It involves exposure to physical sensations that mimic and/or produce symptoms of anxiety and is especially relevant for individuals who have high anxiety sensitivity (i.e., fear of physical symptoms of anxiety; Boswell et al., 2013), such as in the case of panic disorder.

Hierarchy Building

As children learn that treatment involves confronting feared situations, it is important to inform them that exposure does not require facing their greatest fear right away. This can be compared to the unrealistic expectation of jumping into the deep end of a swimming pool before someone knows how to swim. Underscoring the step-by-step process that is utilized to promote their learning and readiness to face their greatest fear fosters their confidence to proceed with treatment. Extending the dog phobia example, children can be asked how they would help a friend to overcome a fear of dogs using the exposure process. Clinicians can offer guidance on the gradual approach that can be taken based on the severity of the fear, such as starting with the word "dog" and then working up to pictures of dogs, a small dog in a cage, a small dog on a leash, and so on. Through this discussion, children can be encouraged to consider what their friend would learn through each incremental step (i.e., that the negative consequences are not happening, that they can handle dogs). This encourages the child's readiness to build their own step-by-step plan to face their fears. This process is called hierarchy building.

During their personalized hierarchy building, the child, clinician, and parent(s) jointly offer ideas to include in the list, and the child is asked to rate the level of fear that s/he anticipates for each step. Hierarchy items or targets should include anxiety triggers, feared outcomes of worries (and situations that activate those fears), and removal of avoidance/safety signals/compulsions. A Subjective Units of Distress Scale (SUDS) or feeling thermometer (e.g., Wagner, 2005) is provided to rate fear intensity, often using a 1 to 10 scale, with 10 being the most intense fear.

Use of visualizations can aid in children's understanding of the hierarchy, especially for younger children, and promote motivation to participate (March & Mulle, 1998). For example, the child's hierarchy can be mapped onto a picture of a stepladder or a swimming pool with visible gradations of depth. It also is helpful to consider ways to personalize the hierarchy. One girl who enjoyed rock wall climbing drew a picture of a wall with grips on a poster and wrote out her hierarchy steps moving up the wall. This encouraged a positive outlook on the exposure process because reaching the top of her hierarchy was represented by her conquering the wall. Another child, a *Lord of the Rings* fan, termed his "the battle for Middle Earth" and mapped out steps in the "Ents (Battle Zone)" (i.e., current working range of anxiety) and "Sauron's Army (future steps)" (i.e., higher level exposures). Other youth-friendly ideas include drawing a treasure map with the top of the hierarchy being the location of the treasure, and using the visual of a basketball court with the opponent's (i.e., anxiety) basket representing the top of the hierarchy. We have also written hierarchy targets on individual strips of paper so that the child could arrange the steps in increasing difficulty to build a ladder that was hung on the wall; this technique adds some increased activity to the hierarchy building process, which can be helpful for younger youth, in particular. This formal structure for the hierarchy encourages the child's confidence and readiness because it ensures a gradual and predictable plan. It also offers an interactive approach with youth physically crossing off or removing their completed exposures as treatment proceeds. See Table 7.1 for an example of a social anxiety hierarchy for an adolescent.

Guidelines for Exposures

Before starting exposure exercises, there are several guidelines to share with youth and their loved ones to encourage a successful response. First, youth need to be aware that feeling anxious is a natural part of the exposure process. In fact, feeling anxious is necessary for learning and habituation to occur. We often use the analogy of jumping into a cold swimming pool to explain the process of feeling distressed in order to promote tolerance and habituation. Most youth can recall the initial discomfort of cold water and how it gets easier—and eventually comfortable—after staying active in the water for a while. We point out that the water temperature has not changed, but their experience of the water has.

Table 7.1 Example of a social anxiety hierarchy

Situation	SUDS (1–10)
Walking through a store	4
Dropping something noisy in public (e.g., keys, coins)	4
Ordering food in restaurant when item is easy to pronounce	4
Answering question in class when confident in the answer	5
Asking for help (e.g., teacher, store assistant)	7
Eating food in public	7
Introducing self to an unfamiliar peer	7–8
Walking through a store and making eye contact	8
Making phone calls	8
Small group activity with peers	8
Starting a conversation with unfamiliar peer	8–9
Ordering food when item is hard to pronounce	9
Reading aloud in a group	9
Making a mistake in conversation	9
Giving a presentation	10

Another guideline to share is how exposures can serve as a structured way to test anxious beliefs and gain corrective information to amend their "false alarm." If we help the child define their testable fear (e.g., "I will be laughed at and rejected if I make a mistake," "I will be attacked by the dog"), then exposures provide the opportunity for corrective learning. Based on the child's age and interests, it may be helpful to describe exposures as "science experiments" where the child is testing specific hypotheses, or as "detective" exercises that help them to "gather clues." It is especially helpful when youth can elicit a "bring it on" attitude that helps them to "poke at" their anxiety, stand up to it, and prove it wrong through the exposure process.

It also is essential that youth and parents are instructed in response prevention (RP; also known as ritual prevention in the context of OCD). RP is defined as resisting safety behaviors, avoidance, and rituals that only offer short-term reduction and neutralization of fear but maintain and even exacerbate the fear response in the long term. Examples of such behaviors include active avoidance of triggers as well as subtle avoidant and safety behaviors (e.g., avoiding eye contact in social situations, always having a parent present in trigger situations) and OCD rituals (e.g., checking, repeating). RP of such behaviors is necessary in order for exposures to generate habituation and extinction of the fear response. It is for this reason that the intervention is called Exposure/Response Prevention (ERP). As a part of this, careful consideration must be taken with parents on identifying patterns of family accommodation (e.g., allowing the child's avoidance, providing reassurance) to ensure that these are addressed and eliminated as a part of RP (Lebowitz et al., 2013). For a more detailed review and description of ERP guidelines, see Abramowitz et al. (2011).

Conducting ERP

Once the foundation is established through education and hierarchy building, the next step involves implementation of the ERP plan. Ideally, the youth is able to complete ERP exercises with the therapist before doing so independently, especially at the outset of treatment and with the more difficult items on their hierarchy. Role-plays can also be used, such as role-playing asking for help in class. Parents are encouraged to observe and learn how to coach their child through the ERP exercises, with the degree of parental involvement based on the child's development and the particular goals. Parents also can assist with the monitoring of ERP completion between sessions and the implementation of a reward system when indicated to promote the youth's motivation. Based on traditional models of ERP (Foa & Kozac, 1986), a general indication that a child has completed an exposure practice is when anxiety has reduced by at least 50 percent based on SUDS ratings. Through prolonged and repeated practice, a hierarchy step is considered mastered when it no longer elicits significant anxiety. A newer model called Inhibitory Learning (Craske et al., 2008), however, underscores the importance of repeated exposure across contexts to promote new learning, regardless of habituation within and between exposures. This model emphasizes the importance of anxiety tolerance in contrast to anxiety reduction.

Given the intricacies of conducting ERP therapy with youth and families, it is recommended that therapists seek formal training. Opportunities for training and consultation can be identified through the Anxiety and Depression Association of America, www.adaa.org, and the Behavior Therapy Training Institute of the International OCD Foundation, www.iocdf.org.

Conclusion

Among the various CBT strategies, ERP is considered a necessary and active component of treatment to promote corrective learning and improve anxiety management. It is through this active process of facing fears that youth learn to overcome their "false alarms." Careful consideration can be taken through psychoeducation and hierarchy building to encourage the youth's understanding and readiness to engage in exposures.

CHAPTER 8

Including the Support System to Enhance Treatment

Parental Involvement

Childhood anxiety affects and is affected by the family system. Parents are in a critical position to positively impact a child's mastery of anxiety management; indeed, parental involvement may enhance treatment outcomes (e.g., Piacentini, Gitow, Jaffer, Graae, & Whitaker, 1994; Waters, Barrett, & March, 2001). In this chapter, we focus on parent characteristics and key ways in which parents can help boost treatment outcomes, including through contingency management to increase youth's active participation and treatment adherence, modeling and coaching of anxiety management skills, reducing family accommodations (FAs), and strategic pressure.

Contingency Management

Studies have shown that transferring active control from therapist to parent, and specifically teaching parents to use contingency management strategies, leads to greater reductions in anxiety following conclusion of active treatment (Manassis et al., 2014). While many anxious youth are motivated for treatment—that is, they want to feel better—practicing new skills and implementing the skills both appropriately and effectively take a lot of effort. Additionally, the intended results (i.e., improved anxiety) do not occur immediately, particularly during exposures, therefore external reinforcers are often quite critical to increase a youth's motivation and encourage adherence. In these instances, reward systems are used to facilitate treatment. For example, a point system may be devised in which a teen earns points for participating in treatment sessions, completing homework assignments daily, and using coping skills in the moment to manage anxiety. Points can be redeemed for a variety of rewards, including those of monetary value as well as extra privileges. Some families agree on certain rewards to be earned contingent upon reaching various treatment goals (e.g., successfully conquering exposures or end of treatment reward). Another example of contingency management is based on the Premack principle in which youth must complete therapy assignments before having access to preferred activities or technology.

In some cases (i.e., more severe symptoms, lower willingness or motivation), rewards may be insufficient. Adding consequences to the contingency management plan is then indicated. Consequences should be based on behaviors as opposed to whether the child feels anxious. Feeling anxious is not a choice; therefore, incurring consequences for feeling anxious would be inappropriate. Behaviors, however, are a choice and within the child's control. As such, consequences can be administered for failing to do certain behaviors or for maladaptive behaviors. For example, we often use time out or job grounding (i.e., a method of discipline in which a child is grounded until a specific chore is completed; Christophersen, 1998) as a consequence for noncompliant and aggressive behavior, regardless of whether those behaviors are driven by anxiety. Other consequences could include fines (i.e., loss of points) or removal of privileges (e.g., phone or social activities) for not completing therapy homework.

Regardless of the specific contingencies implemented, a few key principles will increase the effectiveness of any behavior plan. First, expectations should be clearly defined. The child should know what must be done to earn specific rewards and consequences. Second, consistency is essential. If a child has earned a reward or a consequence, it should be administered. Giving leniency undermines the treatment process. Third, rewards and consequences should fit within the parents' value system. Fourth, adjustments are often necessary to ensure that contingencies remain salient and that expectations are realistic. For example, if a child can earn a highly desirable reward quickly and easily, the reward will lose its value. On the other hand, if a child has to work very hard for an extended period of time to earn a small, minimally preferred reward, the desired motivation enhancement will not be achieved.

Modeling and Coaching

Parents can also help their anxious child through modeling and coaching. Children learn by watching others, and they develop emotion regulation, at least in part, by observing others around them. While parents can inadvertently model anxiety and avoidant coping styles, they also can take advantage of social learning by modeling effective anxiety management. Keeping in mind that children learn best by seeing models struggle and overcome, rather than by seeing a model who never encounters a challenge (Bandura, 1986), parents can model their own coping strategies by first identifying how they are feeling, then making a statement about how they will cope. For example, a parent can say "I'm feeling anxious because I'm worried we're going to be late (identifying feeling). I'm going to take a deep breath and tell myself it's not that big of a deal (coping)." It can be important to include these verbal descriptions as most adaptive coping is done internally, so children do not see the coping process.

Parents can also coach their children in the use of anxiety management skills for practice and "in the moment" application. Teaching a parent how to accurately recognize a child's anxiety and effectively respond to it can increase the likelihood that the child will use new skills when needed. Additionally, providing parents with explicit instructions in what and how to say it, essentially giving them a script, can be helpful.

I can see that your anxiety is going up. Before we do anything, let's do birthday candles breathing. Put your fist up. Here we go . . . Great job! Let's think it through now. What is anxiety telling you? Does that sound like a trick? Can you boss it back? Nicely done!

Family Accommodation

As described in chapter 2, FA is an important aspect to consider. Caregivers are often involved in a child's anxiety disorder symptoms by facilitating avoidance, rituals, and safety behaviors. Examples of common FA are listed in Table 8.1. Failure to reduce or, ideally, eliminate FA will attenuate outcomes.

Table 8.1 Examples of family accommodations

Providing excessive reassurance, answering repeated questions
Making decisions for a child
Speaking for a socially anxious or selectively mute child
Excusing a child's absence from school or picking him up early
Assisting with rituals/following OCD rules
Always accompanying a child to anxiety-provoking places
Sleeping with a child
Limiting social activities to avoid the need for babysitters

Strategic Pressure

Contrary to what many providers believe, a child does not necessarily have to be willing to engage in treatment in order for change to occur. Strategic pressure involves the systematic removal of FA in combination with contingency management strategies. The goal is to extract family members from anxiety disorder-enabling behaviors, which will make it harder for the child to continue to engage in avoidance or ritualizing. Doing so will likely increase the child's discomfort, which in turn may increase motivation for treatment. This approach can be effective when a youth refuses to participate in treatment for any number of reasons including opposition, lack of insight, and low motivation to change.

CHAPTER 9

Including the Support System to Enhance Treatment

Involving the School

Just as parent training is important to a child's anxiety management, seeking active collaboration with the child's school may also be indicated. To determine this, it is important to assess to what extent and in which ways anxiety symptoms may be affecting the child's functioning at school. In some situations, such as in the case of school refusal, the effects of anxiety on school functioning may be obvious. In most circumstances, the interference will be less overt, yet the effects can be similarly detrimental.

Extant research demonstrates that clinical levels of anxiety in youth are negatively associated with academic performance (Langley, Bergman, McCracken, & Piacentini, 2004; Mazzone et al., 2007). In particular, anxiety is related to higher test anxiety, decreased attentional capacity, and poorer recall of previously mastered scholastic knowledge (Ma, 1999). Children may perform well on homework assignments but have trouble demonstrating their knowledge on tests, especially timed tests, due to performance anxiety. They also may avoid asking for help from teachers, or conversely seek excessive reassurance that they are following directions correctly. Anxious children also may have increased somatic complaints with regular requests to visit the nurse's office, and may experience internal restlessness or preoccupations that make it difficult for them to focus in the classroom. Perfectionistic rituals, such as rewriting, rereading, and checking, may also interfere with the child's ability to complete work in a timely, productive manner.

A child's social functioning in school may also be affected by anxiety. As summarized by Wood (2006), highly anxious youth may be overly reticent, avoid peer interactions, or demonstrate less competence around peers due to preoccupations that impair their ability to detect social cues. Indeed, the experience of being surrounded by peers may elevate stress among anxious children (Coplan & Arbeau, 2008). There also may be social fears of negative judgment that contribute to shy and avoidant behaviors and to being perceived by their peers as "unattractive" playmates (Chen, DeSouza, Chen, & Wang, 2006; Gazelle & Ladd, 2003).

Seeking Assistance

Because anxious children generally follow directions and do not exhibit defiant behaviors that draw attention, it is more common for anxiety to go unnoticed by teachers as compared to externalizing conditions. It is therefore helpful for teachers and school staff to become familiar with common signs of anxiety in youth, and for parents and clinicians to engage teachers if anxiety is believed to interfere with the child's school functioning. Active collaboration and assessment among the child's support team (e.g., parents, clinician, teacher(s), school counselor) are important to identify difficulties and inform interventions. Assessment procedures may include a functional analysis completed by the teacher(s), a classroom observation (usually conducted without the child's knowledge), and questionnaires (see Chapter 2).

Accommodations

While anxious youth may highly benefit from accommodations to support successful functioning in the school environment, regular review and modifications are important to encourage a child's progress. For example, a child with social anxiety may be offered the accommodation of only being called on in class when she raises her hand. This structure offers predictability for the child and increased practice using a controlled approach. If this remained stable over time, however, her progress would plateau. As a result, the accommodation must be modified or removed as she shows a readiness for a higher level challenge (i.e., being called on without raising hand) in order to allow for further improvements in her anxiety management and functioning. Of course, careful consideration must be put into the specific modifications and the timing of these changes.

Table 9.1 offers a variety of school-based interventions. Thorough summaries of school-based interventions for youth with anxiety conditions and OCD can be found in Adams (2011) and Reilly (2015).

Table 9.1 Examples of school accommodations

Anxiety concern	Accommodation
Physical restlessness/anxious preoccupations	Movement breaks (e.g., stretching, assisting teachers with errands) Coping break with use of relaxation strategies
Being overwhelmed with tasks	Break assignments into smaller steps
Avoidance and excessive anxiety	Gradual exposure through incremental steps toward facing feared situations
Test anxiety	Coping break before starting test Change format (e.g., from essay to multiple choice) Extended time Quiet, separate location
Anxious preoccupations or transition difficulties	Offer signal before giving instructions Providing a daily schedule
Perfectionism with handwriting	Modifying assignments to reduce workload
Repeated trips to nurse	Coping break location in classroom (e.g., "Relaxation Station" where child can use relaxation strategies) Provide "nurse passes" for day/week; any leftovers "cashed in" for rewards
Social anxiety	Establish a signal to let the student know they are next Use close-ended questions with student Find alternative format for class presentations (e.g., videotape, present to teacher alone)

CHAPTER 10

Putting It All Together

Case Illustrations

Case 1

Maggie

Maggie is an 8-year-old girl who lives with her mother, father, and younger brother. She likes to learn and spend time with her friends. Doing both of these, however, is incredibly difficult for her. When away from her parents, especially at night, Maggie feels extremely sad and nervous. She says that she misses her parents a lot, and she complains of stomachaches every night just before bedtime. She pleads for her parents to lie down with her until she falls asleep. She worries that her parents may die or that someone will kidnap her when she is not with them. Her friends have started to notice that she does not attend dance practice anymore, and they have stopped asking her for playdates and sleepovers because they know she will inevitably decline their invitation. Maggie is embarrassed by her fear and really wants to stay the night with friends. Maggie's symptoms are most consistent with separation anxiety disorder.

Following a comprehensive evaluation to confirm the diagnosis and treatment plan, she and her parents participated in a course of cognitive behavioral therapy. The initial therapy session focused on providing psychoeducation, so that Maggie and her parents were better able to understand the function of anxiety, her disorder, and how avoidance and family accommodation maintain and exacerbate her anxiety disorder symptoms. Externalization was introduced, and Maggie opted to name her anxiety "SAD Man." For homework, Maggie was asked to "be a good spy" and notice when SAD

Man bothered her (i.e., track her anxiety symptoms). In addition, she and her parents brainstormed possible rewards to facilitate treatment adherence (i.e., reward her for being brave). Over the next few sessions, Maggie was taught to use diaphragm breathing to help cope with anxiety-provoking situations and help calm her body at night to prepare for sleep. She was also taught to recognize her thoughts, conceptualized as "SAD Man's tricks and lies" and to "boss them back" (i.e., cognitive restructuring), which was done by role-playing with her therapist first, then her parents, embodying the voice of SAD Man (i.e., vocalizing her anxious thoughts). She also developed a list of coping statements to use when anxious (e.g., "This is a SAD Man trick. I can be brave and bossy! I can handle this!").

The next segment of treatment focused on exposure, introduced as "brave and bossy challenges." Maggie, her parents, and her therapist developed a fear ladder (hierarchy), and it was agreed that she would earn a small reward each time she conquered a rung of her ladder. Maggie's hierarchy included variations of separation as well as removal of family accommodations. Specific targets included: staying with her therapist while parents waited in the waiting room, staying with her therapist while parents left the building to run a short errand, staying with her grandmother during the day for 1 to 2 hours (parents gave her a maximum time rather than a specific time they would be home), falling asleep by herself with agreement that parents would check in on her every 20 minutes, going to sleep by herself without parents checking on her, staying with a babysitter while her parents went out at night, sleeping over at grandmother's house, and sleeping over at a friend's house.

Through these exposure tasks, parents were trained to be effective coaches for Maggie. They prepared her for the exposures by reminding her of the goal and rationale, helping her boss back worries (cognitive restructuring), and reminding her that she can use coping thoughts and breathing to help her cope. As she mastered each exposure as evidenced by little to no reported or observed anxiety or avoidance, they praised her for being brave and gave her the earned reward. Maggie was so excited to be able to do a sleepover with her best friend! To conclude treatment and address relapse prevention, Maggie created an instructional video in which she was the "expert" teaching other children how to manage anxiety.

Case 2

Daryl

Eleven-year-old Daryl is terrified of vomiting since a bout of food poisoning after eating tacos when he was 9 years old. He has refused to eat any Mexican food since then. He also refuses to eat before baseball practice because he is worried that running on a full stomach will make him sick. He often under-eats at meals because feeling full makes him worried that he is going to vomit, and he is timid when brushing his teeth because he does not want to accidentally gag himself. He repeatedly asks others if they are going to get sick if they make comments about not feeling well or say anything about their stomach. He cringes when he hears vomit-related words (e.g., "vomit," "throw up," or "barf") and gets upset when his friends or siblings make gagging sounds, even when joking. He will not watch TV shows or movies if he thinks there may be a vomit scene. Daryl has a specific phobia of vomiting.

Daryl's treatment started with psychoeducation tailored to his specific anxiety presentation. His CBT protocol focused exclusively on exposure, as that is the most effective active treatment component for phobias. Exposure targets included interoceptive exposures (e.g., gagging, drinking water quickly to get the "sloshy" feeling in his stomach, fullness), imaginal exposures (e.g., thinking about getting sick/imagining his worst-case scenario), and *in vivo* exposures (e.g., saying vomit-related words, pictures of vomit, retching sounds, videos of people vomiting, simulating throwing up by kneeling in front of a toilet, spitting out water to simulate vomiting, seeing fake vomit, watching someone realistically simulate getting sick, and simulating throwing up using condensed soup as emesis). As he mastered individual exposure elements, they were combined. That is, he combined imaginal exposure (vivid imagery about getting sick) while inducing his gag response, then pretending to throw up in the toilet.

Daryl willingly engaged in lower level exposures such as pictures, sounds, and imaginal exposures. He had much more difficulty with ones that he thought were "more real" and more likely to result in him actually throwing up. He refused to participate in session, becoming argumentative with his therapist and parents. He also refused to practice exposures outside of session at that point. Parents agreed to implement a reward system in which Daryl was able to earn 5 points each time he completed an exposure; points were redeemable for various privileges and prizes.

Daryl's Reward Menu

Reward	Cost
Dessert	5 points
Stay up 15 minutes later	10 points
Play basketball with dad	10 points
Pick what mom cooks for dinner	10 points
30 extra screen minutes	20 points
Get a new comic book	20 points
Take a friend to the movies	40 points

The implementation of rewards helped increase Daryl's motivation, and he was able to proceed with exposures. He noticed that once he got used to the sensations of gagging and feeling full, his anxiety reduced significantly. He realized that his stomach gives him many signals that do not mean he is going to get sick, whereas prior to treatment any feeling in his stomach (e.g., fullness, hunger, nausea, anxiety) activated his fear. While Daryl says that he still does not want to throw up because "it's gross," he no longer feels afraid.

Case 3

Rick

Rick is 17 years old and painfully shy. Despite feeling completely at ease with his immediate family and long-time friend, Carl, he feels unable to be himself with peers. He worries that he won't be able to come up with anything to say in conversation and that anything he says will sound dumb. When he has tried talking to peers in the past, his mouth has gone dry and his voice felt shaky, which embarrassed him. Participating in class makes him feel nervous, so he usually tries to avoid eye contact or answers teachers' questions with "I don't know." He has not attended a school dance or socialized on the weekend, aside from going to Carl's house, since elementary school. His hair has grown long, not because he prefers it that way but because the idea of going to a hair salon and talking to someone for an extended period of time makes him feel extremely uncomfortable.

Rick lives with his mother and two younger brothers. His mother described Rick as cautious and reserved as early as preschool. He was more social in elementary school, but she noted that he stopped going to birthday parties around 5th grade. Rick disclosed that around that time, he had to read out loud in front of his class. He was really nervous, and he stumbled over his words. A classmate loudly called him stupid, and other peers laughed. His anxiety gradually worsened after that experience.

Rick was very reluctant to participate in therapy and offered little in the way of verbal expression. His therapist hypothesized that his social anxiety interfered. That is, it was hard for him to open up to a new person. Moreover, his fear of negative evaluation was associated with thoughts that there was something fundamentally wrong with him and that his therapist would surely judge him if she knew what was really going on internally. After providing psychoeducation about social anxiety and the tripartite nature of anxiety, his therapist discussed treatment options with Rick and his mother. They decided to pursue a trial of SSRI medication first, with the hope that it would foster his participation in CBT. As his medication was titrated, he continued to meet with his therapist. The first several sessions were focused on increasing Rick's awareness of his symptoms and his understanding of how thoughts, feelings, and behaviors interact. His therapist began to gently challenge some of Rick's anxious thoughts by asking key questions. As Rick became better able to identify his symptoms, cognitive restructuring was introduced. Rick learned common cognitive distortions and was taught to use a thought record in which he focused on identifying his automatic thoughts, evaluating them based on available evidence for accuracy and helpfulness, and generating rational responses. For Rick, it was particularly important for him to practice generating alternative explanations for situations as his automatic thoughts were overly negative and personalized. For example, when he said excuse me to someone who did not respond, Rick thought,

"He is ignoring me because I'm a loser." He was then able to produce an alternative explanation that this person did not respond because Rick's voice volume was low and the venue was noisy. As Rick became more proficient at using cognitive restructuring, therapy shifted to focusing on exposure, which was presented as a behavioral experiment to test out whether anxious predictions are accurate. He practiced tasks such as making phone calls to businesses to ask questions, saying hello to people in the hallway, asking peers questions in class (e.g., to borrow a pen), participating in class by answering questions he was fairly sure he knew the answer to, and going to a football game with Carl but sitting away from the student section.

Rick initially had difficulty with higher level exposures at school because he felt like everyone already knew him as the quiet "loner." He was more willing to test out anxious predictions with strangers who did not know him and he would not see again. For example, he tested out going blank mid-sentence when asking salesclerks questions and realized that, to his surprise, the clerks did not appear to notice. Similarly, he did not get the expected negative reactions when he made verbal mistakes or asked "dumb" questions. With this new information, he was then ready to test out experiments at school, and he practiced striking up conversations with peers. As Rick challenged himself to step out of his comfort zone, in combination with continued medication management, he noticed that his anxiety level decreased and he realized that people do not seem to judge nearly as often as he originally thought. To help him maintain and foster further improvements, he agreed to get a part-time job at a grocery store that would afford him regular opportunities to interact with a variety of people.

CHAPTER 11

Future Directions

As the field of anxiety disorders treatment continues to expand, we anticipate several primary areas of study to enhance the understanding and treatment of anxious youth specifically. One area of increasing interest is a shift from diagnosis-specific treatment to a broader transdiagnostic approach (Ewing, Monsen, Thompson, Cartwright-Hatton, & Field, 2015). This approach underscores the importance of a strong case conceptualization and selection of CBT modules based on a child's symptom profile. This approach has been considered more practical given the high level of comorbidity among disorders and the goal of stronger dissemination of evidence-based treatment.

There also is growing evidence that "third-wave" CBT, which focuses on mindfulness and acceptance-based treatment (e.g., Acceptance and Commitment Therapy), may have clinical utility with anxious youth as well as adult populations. While debate remains in the field whether third-wave treatments represent something truly different or are a repackaging of more conventional CBT, the main difference appears to be that CBT has traditionally aimed at changing maladaptive or distorted thoughts and feelings while newer treatments aim at changing the *relationship* to those same thoughts and feelings.

Investigations of alternative formats for treatment delivery, such as group therapies, telehealth, and self-directed computer-based treatment, are yielding promising results. For example, Lyneham and Rapee (2006) examined the use of bibliotherapy (i.e., self-help book) with therapist support and found this combination, especially when the support was offered by telephone, produced significant results, suggesting that this format may be a viable alternative to traditional face-to-face CBT. Further, technological advances are changing the face of psychological and medical

interventions. Telemedicine, web-based treatments, and apps are regularly being incorporated into treatment. It will be helpful to learn more
about the strengths of using a multimedia approach; certainly, potential
advantages may include greater accessibility of treatment to a wider group
of people and lower financial demands.

References

Abramowitz, J. S., Deacon, B. J., & Whiteside, S. P. (2011). *Exposure therapy for anxiety: Principles and practice.* New York, NY: Guilford Press.

Abramowitz, J. S., Whiteside, S. P., & Deacon, B. J. (2005). The effectiveness of treatment for pediatric obsessive-compulsive disorder: A meta-analysis. *Behavior Therapy, 36,* 55–63.

Adams, G. (2011). *Students with OCD: A handbook for school personnel.* Campton Hills, IL: Pherson Creek Press.

Agency for Healthcare Research and Quality. (2012). Expert consensus guidelines: Practice parameter for the assessment and treatment of children and adolescents with obsessive-compulsive disorder. *Journal of the American Academy of Child & Adolescent Psychiatry, 51,* 98–113.

Albano, A. M., & Kendall, P. C. (2002). Cognitive behavioural therapy for children and adolescents with anxiety disorders: Clinical research advances. *International Review of Psychiatry, 14,* 129–134.

American Academy of Child and Adolescent Psychiatry. (2007). Practice parameter for the assessment and treatment of children and adolescents with anxiety disorders. *Journal of the American Academy of Child & Adolescent Psychiatry, 46,* 267–283.

American Psychiatric Association. (2013). *Diagnostic and statistical manual of mental disorders* (5th ed.). Washington, D.C.: American Psychiatric Publishing.

Anderson, E. A., Smith, A. J., & Christophersen, E. R. (2011). A creative approach to teaching anxiety management skills in children. *The Behavior Therapist, 34,* 3–7.

Antony, M. M., Bieling, P. J., Cox, B. J., Enns, M. W. & Swinson, R. P. (1998). Psychometric properties of the 42-item and 21-item versions of the Depression Anxiety Stress Scale (DASS) in clinical groups and a community sample. *Psychological Assessment, 10,* 176–181.

Baer, S., & Garland, E. J. (2005). Pilot study of community-based cognitive behavioral group therapy for adolescents with social phobia. *Journal of the American Academy of Child & Adolescent Psychiatry, 44,* 258–264.

Ballenger, J. C., Davidson, J. R., Lecrubier, Y., Nutt, D. J., Bobes, J., Beidel, D. C., . . . Westenberg, H. G. (1998). Consensus statement on social anxiety disorder from the international consensus group on depression and anxiety. *Journal of Clinical Psychiatry, 59,* 54–60.

Bandura, A. (1986). *Social foundations of thought and action: A social cognitive theory.* Englewood Cliffs, NJ: Prentice-Hall.

Barrett, P. M. (1998). Evaluation of cognitive-behavioral group treatments for childhood anxiety disorders. *Journal of Clinical Child Psychology, 27,* 459–468.

Barrett, P. M., Rapee, R. M., Dadds, M. M., & Ryan, S. M. (1996). Family enhancement of cognitive style in anxious and aggressive children. *Journal of Abnormal Child Psychology, 24,* 187–203.

Beidel, D. C., & Alfano, C. A. (2011). *Child anxiety disorders: A guide to research and treatment* (2nd ed.). New York, NY: Routledge.

Beidel, D. C., Turner, S. M., & Morris, T. L. (2000). Behavioral treatment of childhood social phobia. *Journal of Consulting and Clinical Psychology, 68,* 1072–1080.

Beidel, D. C., Turner, S. M., Young, B., & Paulson, A. (2005). Social effectiveness therapy for children: Three-year follow-up. *Journal of Consulting and Clinical Psychology, 73,* 721–725.

Berman, S. L., Weems, C. F., Silverman, W. K., & Kurtines, W. M. (2000). Predictors of outcome in exposure-based cognitive and behavioral treatments for phobic and anxiety disorders in children. *Behavior Therapy, 31,* 713–731.

Bernstein, G. A., Borchardt, C. M., Perwien, A. R., Crosby, R. D., Kushner, M. G., Thuras, P. D., & Last, C. G. (2000). Imipramine and cognitive-behavioral therapy in the treatment of school refusal. *Journal of the American Academy of Child & Adolescent Psychiatry, 39,* 276–283.

Biederman, J., Hirshfeld-Becker, D. R., Rosenbaum, J. F., Herot, C., Friedman, D., Snidman, N., . . . Faraone, S. V. (2001). Further evidence of association between behavioral inhibition and social anxiety in children. *The American Journal of Psychiatry, 158,* 1673–1679.

Birmaher, B., Brent, D. A., Chiappetta, L., Bridge, J., Monga, S., & Baugher, M. (1999). Psychometric properties of the Screen for Child Anxiety Related Emotional Disorders (SCARED): A replication study. *Journal of the American Academy of Child and Adolescent Psychiatry, 38,* 1230–1236.

Boswell, J. F., Farchione, T. J., Sauer-Zavala, S., Murray, H. W., Fortune, M. R., & Barlow, D. H. (2013). Anxiety sensitivity and interoceptive exposure: A transdiagnostic construct and change strategy. *Behavior Therapy, 44,* 417–431.

Brown, L. H., Silvia, P. J., Myin-Germeys, I., & Kwapil, T. R., (2007). When the need to belong goes wrong: The expression of social anhedonia and social anxiety in daily life. *Psychological Science, 18,* 778–782.

Burns, D. D. (1980). *Feeling good: The new mood therapy.* New York, NY: William Morrow & Company.

Cartwright-Hatton, S., McNicol, K., & Doubleday, E. (2006). Anxiety in a neglected population: Prevalence of anxiety disorders in pre-adolescent children. *Clinical Psychology Review, 26,* 817–833.

Chambless, D. L., & Hollon, S. D. (1998). Defining empirically supported therapies. *Journal of Consulting and Clinical Psychology, 66,* 7–18.

Chen, X., DeSouza, A., Chen, H., & Wang, L. (2006). Reticent behavior and experiences in peer interactions in Chinese and Canadian children. *Developmental Psychology, 42,* 656–665.

Chorpita, B. F. (2006). *Modular cognitive behavioral therapy for childhood anxiety disorders.* New York, NY: Guilford Press.

Chorpita, B. F., Daleiden, E. L., Ebesutani, C., Young, J., Becker, K. D., Nakamura, B. J., . . . Starace, N. (2011). Evidence-based treatments for children and adolescents: An updated review of indicators of efficacy and effectiveness. *Clinical Psychology Science and Practice, 18,* 154–172.

Christophersen, E. R. (1998). *Beyond discipline: Parenting that lasts a lifetime* (2nd ed.). Shawnee Mission, KS: Overland Press.

Clark, D. A., & Beck, A. T. (2010). *Cognitive therapy of anxiety disorders: Science and practice.* New York, NY: Guilford Press.

Cobham, V. E., Dadds, M. R., & Spence, S. H. (1998). The role of parental anxiety in the treatment of childhood anxiety. *Journal of Consulting and Clinical Psychology, 66,* 893–905.

Compton, S. N., Peris, T. S., Almirall, D., Birmaher, B., Sherrill, J., Kendall, P. C., & Albano, A. M. (2014). Predictors and moderators of treatment response in childhood anxiety disorders: Results from the CAMS trials. *Journal of Consulting and Clinical Psychology, 82,* 212–224.

Coplan, R. J., & Arbeau, K. A. (2008). The stresses of a "brave new world": Shyness and school adjustment in kindergarten. *Journal of Research in Childhood Education, 22,* 377–389.

Coplan, R. J., Prakash, K., O'Neil, K., & Armer, M. (2004). Do you "want" to play? Distinguishing between conflicted shyness and social disinterest in early childhood. *Developmental Psychology, 40,* 244–258.

Costello, E. J., & Angold, A. (1995). Epidemiology. In J. S. March (Ed.). *Anxiety disorders in children and adolescents* (pp. 109–124). New York, NY: Gillford Press.

Craske, M. G., Kitcanski, K., Zelokowsky, M., Mystkowski, J., Chowdhury, N., & Baker, A. (2008). Optimizing inhibitory learning during exposure therapy. *Behavior Research and Therapy, 46,* 5–27.

Davis, T. E., May, A., & Whiting, S. E. (2011). Evidence-based treatment of anxiety and phobia in children and adolescents: Current status and effects on the emotional response. *Clinical Psychology Review, 31,* 592–602.

De Bellis, M. D., Keshavan, M. S., Shifflett, H., Iyengar, S., Dahl, R. E., Axelson, D. A., . . . Ryan, N. D. (2002). Superior temporal gyrus volumes in pediatric generalized anxiety disorder. *Biological Psychiatry, 51,* 553–562.

de Rosnay, M., Cooper, P. J., Tsigaras, N., & Murray, L. (2006). Transmission of social anxiety from mother to infant: An experimental study using a social referencing paradigm. *Behaviour Research and Therapy, 44,* 1165–1175.

di Nardo, P. A., Guzy, L. T., Jenkins, J. A., Bak, R. M., Tomasi, S. F., & Copland, M. (1988). Etiology and maintenance of dog fears. *Behaviour Research and therapy, 26,* 241–244.

Eley, T. C., Rijsdijk, F. V., Perrin, S., O'Connor, T. G., & Bolton, D. (2008). A multivariate genetic analysis of specific phobia, separation anxiety and social phobia in early childhood. *Journal of Abnormal Child Psychology, 36,* 839–848.

Essau, C. A., Conradt, J., & Petermann, F. (2000). Frequency, comorbidity, and psychosocial impairment of anxiety disorders in German adolescents. *Journal of Anxiety Disorders, 14,* 263–279.

Evans, D. W., Gray, F. L., & Leckman, J. F. (1999). The rituals, fears and phobias of young children: Insights from development, psychopathology and neuro-biology. *Child Psychiatry and Human Development, 29,* 261–276.

Ewing, D. L., Monsen, J. J., Thompson, E. J., Cartwright-Hatton, S., & Field, A. (2015). A meta-analysis of transdiagnostic cognitive behavioral therapy in the treatment of child and young person anxiety disorders. *Behavioural and Cognitive Psychotherapy, 43,* 562–577.

Flannery-Schroeder, & Kendall, P. C. (2000). Group and individual cognitive-behavioral treatments for youth with anxiety disorders: A randomized clinical trial. *Cognitive Therapy and Research, 24,* 251–278.

Flavell, J. H., Flavell, E. R., & Green. F. L. (2001). Development of children's understanding of connections between thinking and feeling. *Psychological Science, 12,* 430–432.

Foa, E. B., & Kozak, M. J. (1986). Emotional processing of fear: Exposure to corrective information. *Psychological Bulletin, 99,* 20–35.

Freeman, J., Sapyta, J., Garcia, A., Compton, S., Khanna, M., Flessner, C., & Franklin, M. (2014). Family-based treatment of early childhood obsessive-compulsive disorder: The Pediatric Obsessive-Compulsive Disorder Treatment Study for Young Children (POTS Jr)—a randomized clinical trial. *JAMA Psychiatry, 71,* 689–698.

Gazelle, H. H., & Ladd, G. W. (2003). Anxious solitude and peer exclusion: A diathesis–stress model of internalizing trajectories in childhood. *Child Development, 74,* 257–278.

Garland, E. J., Kutcher, S., Virani, A., & Elbe, D. (2016). Update on the use of SSRIs and SNRIs with children and adolescents in clinical practice. *Journal of the Canadian Academy of Child & Adolescent Psychiatry, 25,* 4–10.

Geller, D., Biederman, J., Jones, J., Park, K., Schwartz, S., Shapiro, S., & Coffey, B. (1998). Is juvenile obsessive-compulsive disorder a developmental subtype of the disorder? A review of the pediatric literature. *Journal of the American Academy of Child & Adolescent Psychiatry, 37,* 420–427.

Gerull, F. C., & Rapee, R. M. (2002). Mother knows best: Effects of maternal modeling on the acquisition of fear and avoidance behaviour in toddlers. *Behaviour Research and Therapy, 40,* 279–287.

Gilbert, A. R., Moore, G. J., Keshavan, M. S., Paulson, L. A., Narula, V., Mac Master, F. P., . . . Rosenberg, D. R. (2000). Decrease in thalamic volumes of pediatric patients with obsessive-compulsive disorder who are taking paroxetine. *Archives of General Psychiatry, 57,* 449–456.

Ginsburg, G. S., & Drake, K. L. (2002). School-based treatment for anxious African-American adolescents: A controlled pilot study. *Journal of the American Academy of Child & Adolescent Psychiatry, 41,* 768–775.

Ginsburg, G. S., Riddle, M. A., & Davies, M. (2006). Somatic symptoms in children and adolescents with anxiety disorders. *Journal of the American Academy of Child & Adolescent Psychiatry, 45,* 1179–1187.

Gonzalez, A., Peris, T. S., Vreeland, A., Kiff, C. J., Kendall, P. C., Compton, S. C., . . . Piacentini, J. (2015). Parental anxiety as a predictor of medication and CBT response for anxious youth. *Child Psychiatry Human Development, 46,* 84–93.

Gordon, J. A., & Hen, R. (2004). Genetic approaches to the study of anxiety. *Annual Review of Neuroscience, 27,* 193–222.

Grayson, J. (2003). *Freedom from obsessive-compulsive disorder: A personalized recovery program for living with uncertainty.* New York, NY: Berkley Books.

Grillon, C., Dierker, L., & Merikangas, K. R. (1997). Startle modulation in children at risk for anxiety disorders and/or alcoholism. *Journal of the American Academy of Child & Adolescent Psychiatry, 36,* 925–932.

Grillon, C., Dierker, L., & Merikangas, K. R. (1998). Fear-potentiated startle in adolescent offspring of parents with anxiety disorders. *Biological Psychiatry, 44,* 990–997.

Guyer, A. E., Lau, J. Y., McClure-Tone, E. B., Parrish, J., Shiffrin, N. D., Reynolds, R. C., . . . Nelson, E. E. (2008). Amygdala and ventrolateral prefrontal cortex function during anticipated peer evaluation in pediatric social anxiety. *Archives of General Psychiatry, 65,* 1303–1312.

Hammad, T. A., Laughren, T., & Racoosin, J. (2006). Suicidality in pediatric patients treated with antidepressant drugs. *Archives of General Psychiatry, 63,* 332–339.

Hayward, C., Killen, J. D., Kraemer, H. C., & Taylor, C. B. (1998). Linking self-reported childhood behavioral inhibition to adolescent social phobia. *Journal of the American Academy of Child & Adolescent Psychiatry, 37,* 1308–1316.

Henry, A., Kisicki, M. D., & Varley, C. (2012). Efficacy and safety of antidepressant drug treatment in children and adolescents. *Molecular Psychiatry, 17,* 1186–1193.

Higa-McMillan, C. K., Francis, S. E., Rith-Najarian, L., & Chorpita, B. F. (2016). Evidence base update: 50 years of research on treatment for child and adolescent anxiety. *Journal of Clinical Child & Adolescent Psychology, 45,* 91–113. doi: http://dx.doi.org/10.1080/15374416.2015.1046177

Hofmann, S. G., & Smits, J. A. (2008). Cognitive-behavioral therapy for adult anxiety disorders: A meta-analysis of randomized placebo-controlled trials. *Journal of Clinical Psychiatry. 69,* 621–632.

Hölzel, B. K., Lazar, S. W., Gard, T., Schuman-Olivier, Z., Vago, D. R., & Ott, U. (2011). How does mindful meditation work? Proposing mechanisms of action from a conceptual and neural perspective. *Perspectives on Psychological Science, 6,* 537–559.

Huebner, D. (2008). *What to do when you dread your bed: A kid's guide to overcoming problems with sleep.* Washington, DC: Magination Press.

In-Albon, T., & Schneider, S. (2006). Psychotherapy of childhood anxiety disorders: A meta-analysis. *Psychotherapy and Psychosomatics, 76,* 15–24.

Jazwierski, Z. (23, August 2013). "Spider-Man: Practicing Mindfulness and Increasing Focus," Kids Relaxation (blog). Retrieved from http://kidsrelaxation.com/uncategorized/spider-man-practicing-mindfulness-and-increasing-focus/

Johnson, S. B., & Melamed. B. G. (1979). The assessment and treatment of children's fears. In B. B. Lahey & A. E. Kazdin (Eds.), *Advances in clinical child psychology* (Vol. 2, pp. 107–139). New York, NY: Plenum Press.

Kabat-Zinn, J. (1994). *Mindfulness meditation for everyday life.* New York, NY: Hyperion.

Kagan, J., Reznick, J. S., & Snidman, N. (1987). The physiology and psychology of behavioral inhibition in children. *Child Development, 58,* 1459–1473.

Keeton, C. P., & Ginsburg, G. S. (2008). Combining and sequencing medication and cognitive-behaviour therapy for childhood anxiety disorders. *International Review of Psychiatry, 20,* 59–164.

Kendall, P. C. (1994). Treating anxiety disorders in children: Results of a randomized clinical trial. *Journal of Consulting and Clinical Psychology, 62,* 100–110.

Kendall, P. C., Brady, E. U., & Verduin, T. L. (2001). Comorbidity in childhood anxiety disorders and treatment outcome. *Journal of the American Academy of Child & Adolescent Psychiatry, 40,* 787–794.

Kendall, P. C., Hudson, J. L., Gosch, E., Flannery-Schroeder, E., & Suveg, C. (2008). Cognitive-behavioral therapy for anxiety disordered youth: A randomized clinical trial evaluating child and family modalities. *Journal of Consulting and Clinical Psychology. 76,* 282–297.

Kendall, P. C., Robin, J. A., Hedtke, K., Suveg, C., Flannery-Schroeder, E., & Gosch, E. (2005). Considering CBT with anxious youth? Think exposures. *Cognitive and Behavioral Practice, 12,* 136–148.

Kendall, P. C., Safford, S., Flannery-Schroeder, E., & Webb, A. (2004). Child anxiety treatment: Outcomes in adolescence and impact on substance use and depression at 7.4-year follow-up. *Journal of Consulting and Clinical Psychology, 72,* 276–287.

Kendall, P. C., & Southam-Gerow, M. A. (1996). Long-term follow-up of a cognitive behavioral therapy for anxiety-disordered youth. *Journal of Consulting and Clinical Psychology, 64,* 724–730.

Kessler, R. C., Chiu, W. T., Demler, O., & Walters, E. E. (2005). Prevalence, severity, and comorbidity of 12-month DSM-IV disorders in the national comorbidity survey replication. *Archives of General Psychiatry, 62,* 617–627.

King, N. J., Eleonora, G., & Ollendick, T. H. (1998). Etiology of childhood phobias: Current status of Rachman's three pathways theory. *Behaviour Research and Therapy, 36,* 297–309.

King, N. J., Muris, P., & Ollendick, T. H. (2005). Childhood fears and phobias: Assessment and treatment. *Child and Adolescent Mental Health, 10,* 50–56.

Koeppen, A. S. (1974). Relaxation training for children. *Elementary School Guidance & Counseling, 9,* 14–21.

Laing, S. V., Fernyhough, C., Turner, M., & Freeston, M. H. (2009). Fear, worry, and ritualistic behaviour in childhood: Developmental trends and interrelations. *Infant and Child Development, 18,* 351–366.

Lang, P. J. (1968). Fear reduction and fear behavior: Problems treating a construct. In J. M. Shlien (Ed.), *The structure of emotion* (pp. 18–30). Seattle, WA: Hogrefe & Huber.

Langley, A. K., Bergman, R. L., McCracken, J., & Piacentini, J. C. (2004). Impairment in childhood anxiety disorders: Preliminary examination of the Child Anxiety Impact Scale–Parent Version. *Journal of Child and Adolescent Psychopharmacology, 14,* 105–114.

Last, C. G., Hersen, M., Kazdin, A., Orvaschel, H., & Perrin, S. (1991). Anxiety disorders in children and their families. *Archives of General Psychiatry, 48,* 928–934.

Last, C. G., & Strauss, C. C. (1989). Obsessive-compulsive disorder in childhood. *Journal of Anxiety Disorders, 3,* 295–302.

Last, C. G., Strauss, C. C., & Francis, G. (1987). Comorbidity among childhood anxiety disorders. *The Journal of Nervous and Mental Disease, 175,* 726–730.

Lazaro, L., Ortiz, A. G., Calvo, A., Ortiz, A. E., Moreno, E., Morer, A., . . . Bargallo, N. (2014). White matter structural alterations in pediatric obsessive-compulsive disorder: Relation to symptom dimensions. *Progress in Neuro-Psychopharmacology and Biological Psychiatry, 54,* 249–258.

Lebowitz, E. R., Woolston, J., Bar-Haim, Y., Calvocoressi, L., Dauser, C., Warnick, E., . . . Leckman, J. F. (2013). Family accommodation in pediatric anxiety disorders. *Depression and Anxiety, 30,* 47–54.

Lebowitz, E. R., & Omer, H. (2013). *Treating childhood and adolescent anxiety: A guide for caregivers.* Hoboken, NJ: John Wiley & Sons.

Lovibond, S. H. & Lovibond, P. F. (1995). *Manual for the Depression Anxiety Stress Scales* (2nd ed.). Sydney, Australia: Psychology Foundation.

Lyneham, H. J., & Rapee, R. M. (2006). Evaluation of therapist-supported parent-implemented CBT for anxiety disorders in rural children. *Behaviour Research and Therapy, 44,* 1287–1300.

Ma, X. (1999). A meta-analysis of the relationship between anxiety toward mathematics and achievement in mathematics. *Journal for Research in Mathematics Education, 30,* 520–540.

Manassis, K., Lee, T. C., Bennett, K., Zhao, X. Y., Mendlowitz, S., Duda, S., & Wood, J. J. (2014). Types of parental involvement in CBT with anxious youth: A preliminary meta-analysis. *Journal of Consulting and Clinical Psychology, 82,* 1163–1172.

Marks, I. M. (1969). *Fears and phobias.* New York, NY: Academic Press.

March, J. S., Biederman, J., Wolkow, R., Safferman, A., Mardekian, J., Cook, E., . . . Wagner, K. D. (1998). Sertraline in children and adolescents with obsessive-compulsive disorder: A multicenter randomized controlled trial. *Journal of the American Medical Association, 280,* 1752–1756.

March, J. S., Frances, A., Carpenter, D., & Kahn, D. A. (n.d.). The expert consensus guideline series: Treatment of obsessive compulsive disorder. Retrieved from http://web.archive.org/web/20070219114941/http://www.psychguides.com/ocgl.html

March, J. S., & Mulle, K. (1998). *OCD in children and adolescents: A cognitive-behavioral treatment manual.* New York, NY: Guilford Press.

Marcus, M. T., Fine, M., Moeller, G., Khan, M. M., Pitts, K., Swank, P. R., & Liehr, P. (2003). Change in stress levels following mindfulness-based stress reduction in a therapeutic community. *Addictive Disorders & Their Treatment, 2,* 63–68.

Masia, C. L., Klein, R. G., Storch, E., A., & Corda, B. (2001). School-based behavioral treatment for social anxiety disorder in adolescents: Results of a pilot study. *Journal of the American Academy of Child & Adolescent Psychiatry, 40,* 780–786.

Mazzone, L., Ducci, F., Scoto, M. C., Passaniti, E., D'Arrigo, V. G., & Vitiello, B. (2007). The role of anxiety symptoms in school performance in a community sample of children and adolescents. *BMC Public Health, 7,* 347. doi:10.1186/1471-2458-7-347

McConaughy, S. (2013). *Clinical interviews for children and adolescents: Assessment to intervention* (2nd ed.). New York, NY: Guilford Press.

McFarlane, A. C. (1987). The relationship between patterns of family interaction and psychiatric disorder in children. *Australian and New Zealand Journal of Psychiatry, 21,* 383–390.

McGuire, J. F., Piacentini, J., Lewin, A. B., Brennan, E. A., Murphy, T. K., & Storch, E. A. (2015). A meta-analysis of cognitive behavior therapy and medication for child obsessive-compulsive disorder: Moderators of treatment efficacy, response and remission. *Depression and Anxiety, 32*, 580–593.

Merikangas, K. R., He, J., Burstein, M., Swanson, S. A., Avenevoli, S., Cui, L., . . . Swendsen, J. (2010). Lifetime prevalence of mental disorders in US adolescents: Results from the National Comorbidity Survey Replication-Adolescent Supplement (NCS-A). *Journal of the American Academy of Child and Adolescent Psychiatry, 49*, 980–989.

Meyer, T. J., Miller, M. L., Metzger, R. L., & Borkovec, T. D. (1990). Development and validation of the Penn State Worry Questionnaire. *Behaviour Research and Therapy, 28*, 487–495.

Moehler, E., Kagan, J., Parzer, P., Wiebel, A., Brunner, R., & Resch, F. (2006). Relation of behavioral inhibition to neonatal and infant cardiac activity, reactivity, and habituation. *Personality and Individual Differences, 41*, 1349–1358.

Monk, C., Kovelenko, P., Ellman, L. M., Sloan, R. P., Bagiella, E., Gorman, J. M., & Pine, D. S. (2001). Enhanced stress reactivity in pediatric anxiety disorders: Implications for future cardiovascular health. *International Journal of Neuropsychopharmacology, 4*, 199–206.

Mowrer, O. R. (1947). On the dual nature of learning: A reinterpretation of 'conditioning' and 'problem-solving.' *Harvard Educational Review, 17*, 102–148.

Muris, P., & Field, A. P. (2008). Distorted cognition and pathological anxiety in children and adolescents. *Cognition and Emotion, 22*, 395–421.

Muris, P., Steerneman, P., Merckelbach, H., & Meesters, C. (1996). The role of parental fearfulness and modeling in children's fear. *Behaviour Research and Therapy, 34*, 265–268.

Ollendick, T. H., & Cerny, J. A. (1981). *Clinical behavior therapy with children.* New York, NY: Plenum.

Ollendick, T. H., & King, N. J. (1998). Empirically supported treatments for children with phobic and anxiety disorders: Current status. *Journal of Clinical Child Psychology, 27*, 156–167.

Ollendick, T. H., King, N. J., & Muris, P. (2002). Fears and phobias in children: Phenomenology, epidemiology, and etiology. *Child and Adolescent Mental Health, 7*, 98–106.

Ollendick, T. H., Matson, J. L., & Helsel, W. J. (1985). Fears in children and adolescents: Normative data. *Behaviour Research and Therapy, 23*, 465–467.

Ollendick, T. H., Yule, W., & Ollier, K. (1991). Fears in British children and their relationship to anxiety and depression. *Journal of Child Psychology and Psychiatry, 32*, 321–331.

Ormel, J., Raven, D., van Oort, F., Hartman, C. A., Reijneveld, S. A., Veenstra, R., . . . Oldehinkel, A. J. (2015). Mental health in Dutch adolescents: A TRAILS report on prevalence, severity, age of onset, continuity and comorbidity of DSM disorders. *Psychological Medicine, 45,* 345–360.

Park, S., Belsky, J., Putnam, S., & Crnic, K. (1997). Infant emotionality, parenting, and 3-year inhibition: Exploring stability and lawful discontinuity in a male sample. *Developmental Psychology, 33,* 218–227.

Peterman, J. S., Carper, M. M., & Kendall, P. C. (2015). Anxiety disorders and comorbid sleep problems in school-aged youth: Review and future research directions. *Child Psychiatry and Human Development, 46,* 376–392.

Piacentini, J., Bennett, S., Compton, S., Kendall, P. C., Birmaher, B., Albano, A. M.,. . .Walkup, J. (2014). 24- and 36-week outcomes for the Child/Adolescent Anxiety Multimodal Study (CAMS). *Journal of the American Academy of Child & Adolescent Psychiatry, 53,* 297–310.

Piacentini, J., Gitow, A., Jaffer, M., Graae, F., & Whitaker, A. (1994). Outpatient behavioral treatment of child and adolescent obsessive compulsive disorder. *Journal of Anxiety Disorders, 8,* 277–289.

Pinto, A., Van Noppen, B., & Calvocoressi, L. (2013). Development and preliminary psychometric evaluation of a self-rated version of the Family Accommodation Scale for Obsessive-Compulsive Disorder. *Journal of Obsessive Compulsive and Related Disorders, 2,* 457–465.

Polanczyk, G. V., Salum, G. A., Sugaya, L. S., Caye, A., & Rohde, L. A. (2015). Annual research review: A meta-analysis of the worldwide prevalence of mental disorders in children and adolescents. *Journal of Child Psychology and Psychiatry, 56,* 345–365.

Pediatric OCD Treatment Study (POTS) Team. (2004). Cognitive-behavior therapy, sertraline, and their combination for children and adolescents with obsessive-compulsive disorder: The Pediatric OCD Treatment Study (POTS) randomized controlled trial. *Journal of the American Medical Association, 292,* 1969–1976.

Qin, S., Young, C. B., Duan, X., Chen, T., Supekar, K., & Menon, V. (2014). Amygdala subregional structure and intrinsic functional connectivity predicts individual differences in anxiety during early childhood. *Biological Psychiatry, 75,* 892–900.

Rachman, S. (1990). The determinants and treatment of simple phobias. *Advances in Behaviour Research and Therapy, 12,* 1–30.

Rapee, R. M. (2003). The influence of comorbidity on treatment outcome for children and adolescents with anxiety disorders. *Behaviour Research and Therapy, 41,* 105–112.

Rapee, R. M., Spence, S. H., Cobham, V., & Wignall, A. M. (2000). *Helping your anxious child: A step-by-step guide for parents.* Oakland, CA: New Harbinger Publications.

Reilly, N. (2015). *Anxiety and depression in the classroom: A teacher's guide to fostering self-regulation in young students.* New York, NY: W. W. Norton & Company.

Rubin, K. H., Hastings, P. D., Stewart, S. L., Henderson, H. A., & Chen, X. (1997). The consistency and concomitants of inhibition: Some of the children, all of the time. *Child Development, 68,* 467–483.

Rynn, M., Puliafico, A., Heleniak, C., Rikhi, P., Ghalib, K., & Vidair, H. (2011). Advances in pharmacotherapy for pediatric anxiety disorders. *Depression and Anxiety, 28,* 76–87.

Salum, G. A., Mogg, K., Bradley, B. P., Gadelha, A., Pan, P. Tamanaha, A. C., . . . Pine, D. (2013). Threat bias in attention orienting: Evidence of specificity in a large community-based study. *Psychological Medicine, 43,* 733–745.

Scahill, L., Riddle, M. A., McSwiggin-Hardin, M., Ort, S. I., King, R. A., Goodman, W. K., . . . Leckman, J. F. (1997). Children's Yale-Brown Obsessive Compulsive Scale: reliability and validity. *Journal of the American Academy of Child & Adolescent Psychiatry, 36,* 844–852.

Schonert-Reichl, K. A., Oberle, E., Lawlor, M. S., Abbott, D., Thomson, K., Oberlander, T. F., & Diamond, A. (2015). Enhancing cognitive and social-emotional development through a simple-to-administer mindfulness-based school program for elementary school children: A randomized controlled trial. *Developmental Psychology, 51,* 52–66.

Schwartz, C. E., Snidman, N., & Kagan, J. (1999). Adolescent social anxiety as an outcome of inhibited temperament in childhood. *Journal of the American Academy of Child & Adolescent Psychiatry, 38,* 1008–1015.

Sheehan, D., Sheehan, K., Douglas Shytle, R., Janavs, J., Bannon, Y., Rogers, J., . . . Wilkinson, B. (2010). Reliability and Validity of the Mini International Neuropsychiatric Interview for Children and Adolescents (MINI-KID). *Journal of Clinical Psychiatry, 71,* 313–326.

Silverman, W. K., & Albino, A. M. (1996). *Anxiety Disorders Interview Schedule for DSM-IV: Child Version.* San Antonio: The Psychological Corp.

Silverman, W. K., Kurtines, W. M., Ginsburg, G. S., Weems, C. F., Lumpkin, P. W., & Carmichael, D. H. (1999). Treating anxiety disorders in children with group cognitive-behavioral therapy: A randomized clinical trial. *Journal of Consulting and Clinical Psychology, 67,* 995–1003.

Silverman, W. K., Pina, A. A., & Viswesveran, C. (2008). Evidence-based psychosocial treatments for phobic and anxiety disorders in children and adolescents. *Journal of Clinical Child & Adolescent Psychology, 37,* 105–130.

Silverman, W. K., Saavedra, L. M., & Pina, A. A. (2001). Test-retest reliability of anxiety symptoms and diagnoses with the Anxiety Disorders Interview Schedule for DSM-IV: Child and Parent Versions. *Journal of the American Academy of Child and Adolescent Psychiatry, 40*(8), 937–944.

Skre, I., Onstad, S., Turgersen, S., Lygren, S., & Kringlen, E. (2000). The heritability of common phobic fear: A twin study of a clinical sample. *Journal of Anxiety Disorders, 14,* 549–562.

Snel, E. (2013). *Sitting still like a frog: Mindfulness exercises for kids (and their parents)*. Boulder, CO: Shambala Publications.

Society of Clinical Child and Adolescent Psychology. (2012). What is evidence-based practice (EBP)? Retrieved from http://effectivechildtherapy .org/content/evidence-based-practice-0

Southam-Gerow, M. A., Kendall, P. C., & Weersing, V. R. (2001). Examining outcome variability: Correlates or treatment response in a child and adolescent anxiety clinic. *Journal of Clinical Child Psychology, 30,* 422–436.

Spence, S. H. (1998). A measure of anxiety symptoms among children. *Behaviour Research and Therapy, 36,* 545–566.

Spence, S. H., Barrett, P. M., & Turner, C. M. (2003). Psychometric properties of the Spence Children's Anxiety Scale with young adolescents. *Journal of Anxiety Disorders, 17,* 605–625.

Spitzer, R. L., Kroenke, K., Williams, J. B., & Lowe, B. (2006). A brief measure for assessing generalized anxiety disorder: The GAD-7. *Archives of Internal Medicine, 166,* 1092–1097.

Spring, B., & Altman. S. (2005). An evidence-based practice glossary: Unscrambling alphabet soup. *The Behavior therapist, 28,* 187–188.

Storch, E. A., Khanna, M. S., Merlo, L. J., Loew, B. A., Franklin, M., Reid, J. M., . . . Murphy, T. K. (2009). Children's Florida Obsessive Compulsive Inventory: Psychometric properties and feasibility of a self-report measure of obsessive-compulsive symptoms in youth. *Child Psychiatry and Human Development, 40,* 467–483.

Storch, E. A., Salloum, A., Johnco, C., Dane, B. F., Crawford, E. A., King, M. A., . . . Lewin, A. B. (2015). Phenomenology and clinical correlates of family accommodation in pediatric anxiety disorders. *Journal of Anxiety Disorders, 35,* 75–81.

Strauss, C. C., Frame, C. L., & Forehand, R. (1987). Psychological impairment associated with anxiety in children. *Journal of Clinical Child Psychology, 16*(3), 235–239.

Strawn, J. R., Welge, J. A., Wehry, A. M., Keeshin, B., & Rynn, M. A. (2015). Efficacy and tolerability of antidepressants in pediatric anxiety disorders: A systematic review and meta-analysis. *Depression and Anxiety, 32,* 149–157.

Suomi, S. J. (1986). Anxiety in young nonhuman primates. In R. Gittelman (Ed.). *Anxiety disorders in childhood* (pp. 1–23). New York, NY: Guillford Press.

Suveg, C., & Zeman, J. (2004). Emotion regulation in children with anxiety disorders. *Journal of Clinical Child and Adolescent Psychology, 33,* 750–759.

Sweeney, M., & Pine, D. (2004). Etiology of fear and anxiety. In T. H. Ollendick & J. S. March (Eds.). *Phobic and anxiety disorders in children and adolescents:*

A clinician's guide to effective psychosocial and pharmacological interventions (pp. 34–60). New York, NY: Oxford University Press.

Turner, S. M., Beidel, D. C., & Costello, A. (1987). Psychopathology in the offspring of anxiety disorders patients. *Journal of Consulting and Clinical Psychology, 55,* 229–235.

Turner, S. M., Beidel, D. C., & Larkin, K. T. (1986). Situational determinants of social anxiety in clinic and nonclinic samples: Physiological and cognitive correlates. *Journal of Consulting and Clinical Psychology, 54,* 523–527.

Turner, S. M., Beidel, D. C., & Roberson-Nay, R. (2005). Offspring of anxious parents: Reactivity, habituation, and anxiety-proneness. *Behaviour Research and Therapy, 43,* 1263–1279.

Uher, R., Heyman, I., Turner, C. M., & Shafran, R. (2008). Self-, parent-report and interview measures of obsessive-compulsive disorder in children and adolescents. *Journal of Anxiety Disorders, 22,* 979–990.

Vicente, B., Saldivia, S., de la Barra, F., Kohn, R., Pihan, R., Valdivia, M., . . . Melipillan, R. (2012). Prevalence of child and adolescent mental disorders in Chile: A community epidemiological study. *Journal of Child Psychology and Psychiatry, 53,* 1026–1035.

Wagner, A. P. (2003). Cognitive-behavioral therapy for children and adolescents with obsessive-compulsive disorder. *Brief Treatment and Crisis Intervention, 3,* 291–306.

Wagner, A. P. (2005). *Worried no more: Help and hope for anxious children.* Rochester, NY: Lighthouse Press.

Wagner, A. P. (2013). *Up and down the worry hill: A children's book about obsessive compulsive disorder and its treatment* (3rd ed.). Rochester, NY: Lighthouse Press.

Walkup, J. T., Albano, A. M., Piacentini, J., Birmaher, B., Compton, S. N., Sherrill, J. T., . . . Kendall, P. C. (2008). Cognitive behavioral therapy, sertraline, or a combination in childhood anxiety. *The New England Journal of Medicine, 359,* 2753–2766.

Waters, T. L., Barrett, P. M., & March. J. S. (2001). Cognitive-behavioral family treatment of childhood obsessive-compulsive disorder: Preliminary findings. *American Journal of Psychotherapy, 55,* 372–387.

Watson, J. B., & Rayner, R. (1920). Conditioned emotional reactions. *Journal of Experimental Psychology, 3,* 1–14.

Willard, C. (2010). *Child's mind: Mindfulness practices to help our children be more focused, calm, and relaxed.* Berkeley, CA: Parallax Press.

Williams, J. M., Matthews, A., & MacLeod, C. (1996). The emotional stroop task and psychopathology. *Psychological Bulletin, 120,* 3–24.

Wood, J. (2006). Effect of anxiety reduction on children's school performance and social adjustment. *Developmental Psychology, 42,* 345–349.

Wood, J. J., Piacentini, J. C., Southam-Gerow, M., Chu, B. C., & Sigman, M. (2006). Family cognitive behavioral therapy for child anxiety disorders. *Journal of the American Academy of Child & Adolescent Psychiatry, 45,* 314–321.

Woodward, L. J., & Fergusson, D. M. (2001). Life course outcomes of young people with anxiety disorders in adolescence. *Journal of the American Academy of Child & Adolescent Psychiatry, 40,* 1086–1093.

Zoogman, S., Goldberg, S. B., Hoyt, W. T., & Miller, L. (2014). Mindfulness interventions with youth: A meta-analysis. *Mindfulness, 6,* 290–302.

Author Biography

Ashley J. Smith, PhD, began studying and treating anxious youth while pursuing her PhD in Clinical Psychology. She earned her doctorate with an emphasis in children and families from the University of Nebraska-Lincoln. She completed an APA-approved predoctoral internship at Children's Mercy Hospital and Clinics before joining the staff at Omaha Children's Hospital to help develop their dedicated anxiety services. After two years, she relocated to Kansas City to serve as a senior staff psychologist at the Kansas City Center for Anxiety Treatment, P.A. for over seven years before starting a private practice. She provides evidence-based assessment and treatment for anxiety and obsessive compulsive spectrum disorders across the life span, with expertise in Cognitive Behavioral Therapy. Dr. Smith has served as an Adjunct Assistant Professor in the Department of Psychology at the University of Missouri-Kansas City and has provided supervision and consultation for trainees and other clinicians. She has several previous research and clinically focused publications. She maintains active involvement in professional organizations and regularly presents workshops and trainings on a local and national level.

Amy M. Jacobsen, PhD, received her PhD in Clinical Psychology from The University of Georgia, with specific emphases in child psychology and the study and treatment of anxiety disorders. She completed her internship in Clinical Psychology at SUNY Upstate Medical University followed by a 2-year APA-accredited postdoctoral fellowship in Clinical Child Psychology at Mayo Clinic in Rochester, Minnesota. She has served as an Assistant Professor in the Mayo Clinic College of Medicine, a Research Assistant Professor in the Department of Neurology at Hoglund Brain Imaging Center/University of Kansas Medical Center, and an Adjunct Assistant Professor in the Department of Psychology at the University of Missouri, Kansas City. She worked as a senior staff psychologist at the Kansas City Center for Anxiety Treatment, P.A. for over seven years. She currently has a private practice within InSight Counseling, LLC where she works with individuals across the life span and specializes in the full range of Cognitive Behavioral Therapy services for anxiety disorders and obsessive compulsive spectrum conditions. Dr. Jacobsen has published several research articles and presents at state and national organizations. She also serves as the president of OCD Kansas, Inc., a nonprofit organization affiliated with the International Obsessive Compulsive Disorder Foundation.

Index

OTHER TITLES IN OUR CHILD CLINICAL PSYCHOLOGY "NUTS AND BOLTS" COLLECTION

Samuel T. Gontkovsky, *Editor*

- *Learning Disabilities* by Charles J. Golden and Lisa K. Lashley
- *Intellectual Disabilities* by Charles J. Golden and Lisa K. Lashley
- *A Guide for Statistics in the Behavioral Sciences* by Jeff Foster
- *Childhood Sleep Disorders* by Connie J. Schnoes
- *Childhood and Adolescent Obesity* by Lauren A Stutts
- *Elimination Disorders: Evidence-Based Treatment for Enuresis and Encopresis* by Thomas M. Reimers
- *Depression in Childhood and Adolescence: A Guide for Practitioners* by Rebecca A. Schwartz-Mette, Cynthia A. Erdley, Douglas W. Nangle and Hannah Lawrence

Momentum Press offers over 30 collections including Aerospace, Biomedical, Civil, Environmental, Nanomaterials, Geotechnical, and many others. We are a leading book publisher in the field of engineering, mathematics, health, and applied sciences.

Momentum Press is actively seeking collection editors as well as authors. For more information about becoming an MP author or collection editor, please visit http://www.momentumpress.net/contact

Announcing Digital Content Crafted by Librarians

Concise e-books business students need for classroom and research

Momentum Press offers digital content as authoritative treatments of advanced engineering topics by leaders in their field. Hosted on ebrary, MP provides practitioners, researchers, faculty, and students in engineering, science, and industry with innovative electronic content in sensors and controls engineering, advanced energy engineering, manufacturing, and materials science.

Momentum Press offers library-friendly terms:
- *perpetual access for a one-time fee*
- *no subscriptions or access fees required*
- *unlimited concurrent usage permitted*
- *downloadable PDFs provided*
- *free MARC records included*
- *free trials*

The **Momentum Press** digital library is very affordable, with no obligation to buy in future years.

For more information, please visit **www.momentumpress.net/library** or to set up a trial in the US, please contact **mpsales@globalepress.com**.